SECTIONS AND POLITICS

Photo: Harold Hone

WILLIAM B. HESSELTINE

SECTIONS
and
POLITICS

SELECTED ESSAYS BY

WILLIAM B. HESSELTINE

Edited with an Introduction by

RICHARD N. CURRENT

MADISON : MCMLXVIII

STATE HISTORICAL SOCIETY OF WISCONSIN

INTRODUCTION

A FIRST encounter with Professor Hesseltine could be a terrifying experience, at least for a youthful student approaching him in his Bascom Hall office. The professor was so short that his head did not extend much above the back of the swivel chair in which, his stubby legs crossed, he sat tilted rearward at a precarious angle. Yet he loomed like an ogre. He seemed ageless, unborn and undying, a venerable institution, even at a time when he was still in his thirties. Before responding to the excuses of his visitor, he fixed upon him for a while an unrelenting stare. He took from his mouth a curved-stem pipe, which had gone out again, and held it in his right hand. He passed the other hand lightly across his bald dome, and his heavy mustache twitched once or twice, almost imperceptibly. When he finally spoke, his words came rumbling up as if from a cavernous depth; his voice must have been a full octave lower than that of any other member of the Wisconsin faculty. What he proceeded to say, as well as the way he said it, was memorable. Gruffly, he got to the point, with few of the circumlocutions that professors customarily use in reproving their students.

His students knew him as a lively if eccentric performer in the lecture hall—especially the undergraduates who, four or five hundred at a time, took the United States history survey course. While giving them plenty of substance, he put it in a form that made it highly palatable. At times he orated with an air of mock pomposity, and at other times he chatted as if reminiscing of men and events he personally had known, but all the while he was showing the relevance of the past to the present. He scattered home-made epigrams right and left as he went along. "Conservatives opposed the Declaration of Independence as much in 1776 as they do now." "Jefferson in the White House could afford the appearance of simplicity. There was no Mrs. Jefferson to insist on giving teas." " 'Aristocrats' arose quickly on the frontier. But 'aristocracy' was unpopular, and so everyone talked 'democracy.' " "Lincoln's personality was repulsive to pompous men." "Note that F. D. R., when he speaks of great Democrats, never mentions Cleveland. Cleveland was a Republican in sheep's clothing." Sometimes he taught by indirection, or even by what might be called the reverse method, asserting the opposite of what he really meant, so as to shock his hearers into thinking for themselves. With a straight face he once contended, for example, that the economic and social ills of the Great Depression could be cured by reintroducing slavery and applying it to white as well as Negro workers. His lectures seldom were models of organization, and even bright students might occasionally find him confusing. But only dullards ever found him dull.

His seminar was a startling but rewarding school for historical scholars. A young man or woman coming into it from the didactic atmosphere of the usual undergraduate class, or transferring to it from the coldly formal air of some other university seminar, might not know at first what to make of the din and disorder that often prevailed here. These weekly get-togethers in the late afternoon might turn into what seemed like dramatic happenings. No one knew just what to expect, though each had his assignment. But everyone could be sure of intellectual excitement to be aroused by the improvising professor, who could easily prod his students into rebutting him or disputing with one another. He obviously enjoyed the sessions, and the sharper the verbal combat, the better he liked it. (He had told his first group of Wisconsin students, at their very first meeting, that the best seminar was like a dogfight.) These meetings were much more than the wind-beating affairs they might have appeared to a casual visitor. The professor was teaching all the time.

He was teaching curiosity and enthusiasm about history, caution as well as imagination in interpreting the records of the past, and concern for presenting one's findings in good, readable prose. Curiosity he aroused by tossing out generalizations that defied common knowledge or common sense. After testing a few of these, his students might find them as insubstantial as they were outlandish, or as perceptive as they were original. In either case, the students learned something about the kinds of questions that might be asked and answered through historical study. Caution he instilled by urging his students to doubt every document and assume that every witness was a damned liar. He suggested that the statements of politicians, instead of being taken at face value, ought to be treated much like the works of fictionists and subjected to a comparable kind of literary criticism. Concern for historical composition he encouraged with this advice to his Ph. D. candidates: "Write a book, not a dissertation." Modest in his own pretensions as a writer, he was quick to recognize the promise of writing ability in his students, and as quick to correct their tendencies toward what he considered poor style. He presented a list of literary commandments, one of which was "Thou shalt not use the passive voice." Arbitrary though such injunctions might seem, they did what they were intended to do. They warned budding historians against the perils of flabby construction, mindless rhetoric, and dissertationese.

Not all survived the seminar. Some never overcame the

bafflement they ran into at the very beginning. Others succumbed to a terror of the Hesseltine presence. The great majority, however, not only stayed on but soon began to feel a deep affection mingled with their awe. To at least a few he became a kind of god.

Once a student had finally got his doctoral degree, the professor accepted him cordially as a friend and fellow historian. Still, the new doctor hardly knew quite how to treat the older one, or even quite how to address him. If the professor sent him a letter—typed on a scrap of yellow paper, like as not, or on some fugitive piece of hotel stationery—it invariably bore the typewritten signature "wbh," without periods or capitals. Those initials, though they served well enough for the salutation in a written reply, would hardly do when one was addressing him in person. "Bill," as he was known to his colleagues, was much too familiar a form for any except the boldest of the young Ph. D.'s. "Best," as he was known to his wife, was too intimate for any of them. Most continued, as before, to call him "Dr. Hesseltine." And those of the early generations pronounced the name "Hess'-l-tyne," with a sibilant "s" and a long "i." Some of the later comers said "Hezz'-l-teen," which is the pronunciation he himself indicated in his *Who's Who* sketch, though he was never known to correct anyone who pronounced it the other way.

All looked to him for aid in getting a job, and then for further help in securing a better one, and seldom did they look in vain. He watched closely the careers of his former students, taking pride in their advancement. On shelves of honor in his study at home he kept the books of those who published. He himself had something to do with many of these volumes, and not only with those that were derived from dissertations, for his teachings continued to condition the point of view from which his former students wrote. His

example also influenced their teaching in their own classrooms. They reused his ideas, retold his stories, and even
imitated as best they could his mannerisms. Eventually,
most of them broke away from the Hesseltine pattern and
began to mature along the lines of their separate interests
and personalities. This might require some effort. He had
not set out deliberately to make himself a guru, with disciples attached to him, yet he tended to do that unintention-
ally through the charismatic effect he had upon a number
of his students. Even after setting an independent course for
themselves, they seldom could quite put aside the Hesseltine
manner; they could not always even recognize its continuing
presence. Consciously or not, they incorporated Hesseltin-
isms in their lectures and thus handed them down to their
students, who later repeated them to *theirs,* with all the
freshness of originality.

His colleagues in the history department at Wisconsin,
whatever the differences that some had with him, recognized
him as one devoted to the best interests of the department
as a whole. In its closed meetings he seldom hesitated to
express dissenting views when he had them. He put them
forthrightly. Once the majority had made its decision, however, he loyally supported the departmental policy, whether
it accorded with his recommendations or not. He never
carried internal controversies, or even exposed them, to the
university world outside. With the passage of time, and the
retirement or death of older members, he emerged as the
elder statesman of the department. He became the reposi-
tory of its constitutional lore, the man to whom others
turned for ancient precedents and forgotten rules. With the
swelling university enrollments, the crowding of Bascom
offices and classrooms, and the scattering of history classes all
over the broad campus, he took upon himself the leadership
of a campaign to provide a new and adequate history build-

ing. With characteristic whimsy, he once put in a requisi-
tion, of the kind used to order such things as note pads and
pencils, for "One history building—$1,000,000." The edi-
fice that finally arose, or that portion of it allotted to the
history department, could appropriately have been named
(though it was not) Hesseltine Hall.

To his friends he was the soul of hospitality, the perfect
host along with his wife, who was the perfect hostess. He
and Katherine might briefly have bewildered a stranger as
the two of them exchanged insults in front of their guests,
but even the newcomer would soon realize that this was affec-
tionate banter, a demonstration not of disagreement but of
close communion and true understanding. The Hesseltines
shared, among other things, a sense of humor, and she often
acted as a willing foil for his jokes. He (and she as well) was
always glad to hear a new story—broad or not, so long as it
was funny—and if it was good enough he jotted down the
key words in a little pocket notebook. He would even rather
tell than hear a story, and he told it like a master raconteur,
holding the complete attention of his audience, while he
commanded them with his twinkling brown eyes. As a
raconteur, though, he was much more than an expert re-
teller of tales. He also made up humorous anecdotes from
his own experiences and came forth with novel commen-
taries on passing events. His friends would await his report
on some occurrence they themselves had observed or taken
part in—so as to find out what unimagined drama, paradox,
or irony remained to be revealed about it. From him they
expected the unexpected, and they were seldom disap-
pointed.

Even those who had been acquainted with him for
twenty-five or thirty years were often hard put to know
when he was joking and when he meant to be taken seriously. One thing at least he was completely in earnest about.

Though a man of peace, he continually carried on a war of his own, a war against the jejune, the pretentious, and the sham.

His conversational interests ranged widely, with or without a glass of bourbon and branch water in his hand. He had an opinion, an original one, on practically everything relating to this world or the next, except music. He was tone deaf. Much of the stuff of his conversation he derived from his travels. Good traveler that he was, he brought a treasure of experience back from the states and countries he visited, because he had carried a treasure of experience to them. He was discriminating, though. At one American tourist spot, where visitors were asked to record their impressions of the place, he and Katherine were captivated by the comment that someone had written down: "Interesting and educational." The Hesseltines promptly adopted this phrase, though not in quite the sense of their predecessor; they used it to characterize the sights they considered hardly worth seeing.

He was more than good company. He was the best of friends. For all the gruff exterior that he liked to put on, he was warmth and gentleness and kindliness within. He made enemies, as anyone so crotchety and so outspoken was bound to do, but he made vastly more friends, unnumbered friends, in Madison and everywhere he went.

The end came without warning. True, he had a background of high blood pressure, which made him uninsurable, and a few years before his death he had undergone a serious operation, in which a kidney was removed. Still, to those around him, he seemed somehow indestructible. On the last afternoon he appeared to be in unusually good form, as he made his way through the crowd at the president's cocktail party, from time to time putting his glass of bourbon in the side pocket of his jacket, so as to free both hands while he refilled and relit his pipe. At dinner that evening he regaled his companions, as usual. The next morning it was hard—it was impossible—to believe that he was really dead, the victim of a massive cerebral hemorrhage. And even after the funeral some of his friends had to repress the expectation of listening to his inimitable commentary once again. What would *he* have had to say about the funeral?

* * * *

William Best Hesseltine died in Madison, Wisconsin, on December 8, 1963. He had been born in Brucetown, Virginia, a hamlet in the northernmost corner of the state, near the West Virginia line, on February 21, 1902.

He was the only child of William Edward, who had married rather late in life, and Rosa May (Best) Hesseltine. The father, a sea captain, spent most of his time on distant voyages. He died of a heart attack in San Francisco, as he was about to take a ship to South America, when his son was only a few years old. The boy had little or no memory of his father and, after his mother remarried, little or nothing in common with his stepfather. Running away from home, young William finally found refuge with an uncle and an aunt, Colonel and Mrs. Carl Best. Colonel Best, a graduate of the Virginia Military Institute, owned and operated a boarding school for boys, the Millersburg Military Institute, in northern Virginia.

The vicinity of Hesseltine's birth and upbringing, in the Valley of Virginia, contained such historic spots as Harpers Ferry and Winchester. It had been the scene of much regular and irregular fighting during the Civil War, and allegiances there had been uncertainly divided as between the Union and the Confederacy. During his boyhood the older folks could still recall the war time, and they often did, as if it had been yesterday. One of his grandfathers, affectionately known throughout the countryside as "the crazy little doctor," had refused to fight or speak for either side but had gone about his business of caring for the sick and wounded, Yankee and Rebel alike. From the recollections of this grandfather and other elders in the neighborhood, and from visits to the battlefields thereabout, young Hesseltine received his earliest impressions of the historic past. He also derived the interest that was eventually to turn him into an historian.

After graduating from his uncle's proprietary academy, Hesseltine at the age of sixteen went off to Lexington, but not to enroll in the uncle's alma mater, the Virginia Military Institute. He chose Washington and Lee University instead. There he joined the Theta Chi fraternity and, while still a sophomore, began to court a Lexington girl, Katherine Kramer. He also found time to make an excellent record as a student, winning election to the local chapter of Phi Beta Kappa. He was awarded the bachelor of arts degree in the spring of 1922. That fall, he commenced his teaching career as a teacher of history and geography at the University Military School in Mobile, Alabama, where he remained for only one academic year.

On September 1, 1923, he and Katherine Kramer were married, and he took his bride with him to his next job, with the title of professor of history and social sciences, at Scarrit-Morrisville College, in Morrisville, Missouri. After a year there, he spent two years at the University of Arkansas as an instructor in history. Meanwhile, during his summer vacations, he attended the University of Virginia as a graduate student. With a thesis entitled "Belligerent Rights as Applied by Napoleon III to the Southern Confederacy," he earned the master's degree in 1925.

In 1926 the Hesseltines, continuing their itinerant life, moved from Fayetteville, Arkansas, to Columbus, Ohio, where he entered the graduate school of the Ohio State University. They now had two children: William, about a year and a half; and Katherine, only a few months old. Somehow the family managed to survive on his modest stipend as a teaching assistant. In those days Ohio State boasted a distinguished history faculty, numbering among others Arthur Charles Cole, Homer C. Hockett, and Carl Wittke. Cole, a Civil War expert then just turning forty, was Hesseltine's major professor and exerted the greatest influence upon him. Hockett, in his early fifties, was also influential, and so, to a less extent, was Wittke, who was the head of the department though still in his mid-thirties. Writing his dissertation on Civil War prisons, Hesseltine obtained his doctorate of philosophy in 1928, at the age of twenty-six.

Dr. Hesseltine immediately took a position as professor of history at the University of Chattanooga. While there, he became a friend of the local newspaperman George Fort Milton, who was at work on his biography of Stephen A. Douglas. He also made himself familiar with Lookout Mountain and Missionary Ridge, acquiring a first-hand knowledge of the lay of the land, knowledge that he was to incorporate in a classic lecture on the Battle of Chattanooga. He was completing his fourth year at Chattanooga when, in the spring of 1932, an opening suddenly appeared at the University of Wisconsin through the untimely death of Carl Russell Fish, a very popular lecturer and a noted Civil War historian (as well as an authority on American diplomatic history).

Hesseltine, youthful though he was, already had a reputation, spreading beyond the Chattanooga area, as a favorite with both students and the public. Over the local radio he had presented a series of sketches of American statesmen from Benjamin Franklin to Robert E. Lee, which the university of Chattanooga published as a booklet, *Twelve Rep-*

resentative Americans (1930). This little volume, "with its impressionistic touches at times given in quite too bold strokes," the *Mississippi Valley Historical Review* noted, "suggests the usefulness of the trained historian as the popularizer of historical material." More to the point, he had to his credit a half-dozen scholarly articles and a substantial monograph, his doctoral dissertation, *Civil War Prisons* (The Ohio State University Press, 1930). One scholarly reviewer hailed this as "an exhaustive, impartial, and critical study," and another commended the author for his "judicial spirit and cool detachment." He also had a contract for a volume on the political career of Ulysses S. Grant, to be published in Dodd, Mead and Company's American Political Leaders series. When he received the offer from Wisconsin, he gladly accepted it, even though this meant a reduction in rank from professor to assistant professor.

The Wisconsin department of history, traditionally one of the strongest in the country, particularly with regard to the American field, was facing a crisis in 1932. It had lost its "big three" in American history: Fish, Winfred T. Root, and Frederick L. Paxson. At the time of Fish's death, Root had already left for Iowa, and Paxson had decided to go to Berkeley. As Root's successor, Curtis P. Nettels had been in Madison for a couple of years. Now, at the same time as Hesseltine arrived to take Fish's place, John D. Hicks appeared as a full professor to take Paxson's. Of Hesseltine, Hicks afterward wrote: "Bill and I became devoted friends, and remained so for all the rest of his life, although we disagreed violently on nearly every important issue, whether related to historical interpretation or to current events." It might be added that the relationship between Hesseltine and Nettels was practically the reverse: they held similar views on many historical and contemporary questions but were not very compatible personally or socially. Yet all three worked together to maintain and improve the work of the department, under the leadership of its great chairman, Paul Knaplund, whom Hesseltine always respected and admired.

During the more than thirty-one years that Hesseltine remained a member of the department, its composition and his role underwent considerable changes. After four years he was promoted to an associate professorship, and after four more, to a full professorship. Eventually Hicks and Nettels departed, and more and more new Americanists arrived, until their number was five or six times as large as it had been, and the teaching in American and other fields was much more highly specialized. At first, Hesseltine taught a two-semester course on the sectional controversy and another on constitutional history, in addition to his seminar. Then, inheriting from Hicks the survey course, which Hicks had inherited from Fish, he taught this also while alternating his two advanced lecture courses. Later he turned over to others both the constitutional history and the survey, but from time to time he offered (perhaps his own favorite) a biographical approach to the American past, which he called "Representative Americans." Still later, he graciously yielded to a new colleague the second semester of his course on the sectional controversy ("Reconstruction and the New Nation"), and finally the other half ("Sectionalism and the Civil War") as well. By that time he held a chair as William F. Vilas Research Professor of History, to which he was appointed in 1962, with only such teaching duties as he might choose. He chose to continue his seminar and a course in historical writing, intended for students who had already written substantial essays and wished to put them into shape for publication.

Much the largest share of Hesseltine's instructional time went to his seminar students, the authors of the theses and dissertations that he supervised. A total of thirty-two of his students completed the work for the Ph. D., and a great many more for the M. A. Practically all of them wrote on topics having to do with the Civil War or with Reconstruction. In reading and criticizing seminar papers and other drafts, he was almost always thorough, meticulous, unsparing, and often whimsically humorous besides. He never assigned or approved topics that would provide material for his own projects. He meant for his students to have their work published under their names, if it was worth publishing. To facilitate the publication of master's and doctor's essays, in cases where the length or subject, though not the quality, made it difficult to find publishers, he started the Logmark series of slim volumes, set up by typewriter, reproduced by photoprint, and issued by the history department in co-operation with the State Historical Society of Wisconsin.

Hesseltine carried his provocative influence as a lecturer far beyond the Wisconsin campus, addressing as many as two to four dozen groups a year, in Wisconsin and throughout the country. He appeared before both academic and non-academic audiences, among them women's societies, service clubs, and Civil War amateurs. He was a charter member and guiding spirit of the Madison Civil War Round Table, and he was also a leader of the Lincoln Fellowship of Wisconsin. In addition to his many brief visits to other campuses, including an appearance as the Walter Lynwood Fleming Lecturer at Louisiana State University (1949), he made longer sojourns as a visiting professor at New York University (1939), Rice University (1953–1954), Stanford University (1954), and the University of South Carolina (1957).

He also lectured widely abroad. Going first to England, he served (1945) on the faculty of the temporary university

set up at Shrivenham for American soldiers awaiting their
return home after World War II. In Costa Rica, Honduras,
and Guatemala he delivered a succession of public addresses
(1947). In Germany he presided over a German-American
historical conference at Braunschweig and spoke to university groups elsewhere (1955). In Iran, Afghanistan,
Pakistan, and Ceylon he appeared before a variety of audiences as an American Specialist under the auspices of the
State Department, to assist in the celebration of the sesqui-
centennial of Lincoln's birth (1959). In India he attended
the Mussoorie conference on American studies (1963) and
had an important part in the founding of what was to become the Indian Congress of American History.

While a conscientious teacher and a wide-ranging lecturer, Hesseltine remained an industrious scholar also. He
saw no contradiction between good teaching and productive
scholarship. Quite the contrary. To quote from an article he
once wrote (1942) in collaboration with Louis Kaplan:

> From the first years of the Ph. D. in America, a curious
> controversy between "teaching" and "research" has waxed
> and waned in academic circles. The fact that a majority of
> doctors of philosophy have entered college teaching has
> given plausibility to perennial demands from college ad-
> ministrators, educationists, and journalistic pundits that
> the universities should train teachers rather than re-
> searchers. Apparently the critics of the Ph. D. program,
> deceived by their own words, fail to perceive that teach-
> ing and learning are one and the same thing. The college
> teachers who are not actively engaged in contributing to
> their own knowledge and testing the results of their own
> researches are failing in their duty to their college, their
> students, and their profession.
>
> The college official who fails to encourage his faculty's
> researches or who emphasizes that he is seeking "good
> teachers, not research men," may be protecting his
> budget, but he is defrauding his patrons.

Living up to his own ideal of the scholar-teacher, Hesseltine produced all together a dozen books, edited or helped to edit five others, turned out by himself or with a collaborator more than a hundred articles (not counting numerous contributions to encyclopedias), and wrote nearly four hundred book reviews.

Many of his articles were tendentious and dealt with contemporary rather than historical subjects—aspects of the New Deal, World War II, postwar policies, and so on—for he was a propagandist and pamphleteer as well as an historian and educator. A good friend of Morris Rubin and Mary Sheridan, editors of *The Progressive,* he was for many years a fairly regular contributor to that magazine. He also contributed to the *New Leader* and to the *Milwaukee Journal,* the *Chicago Tribune,* and other newspapers.

Virginian though he was by birth and background, he naturalized himself as a good Wisconsinite. He became devoted to the interests and the history of his adopted state. He maintained and encouraged the long-standing special relationship between the history department and the State Historical Society of Wisconsin, as, for example, in promoting the co-operative publishing venture of the Logmark series. He willingly served as a member of the Society's board of curators and (1961–1963) as its president. Little interested in the museum aspect of the Society's work, he emphasized its scholarly functions and did all he could to further its collecting and publishing activities. "We all teach Wisconsin history," he once remarked with regard to the American historians at the university. Certainly, he himself in his lecture courses illustrated national developments with local references, and in his seminar he urged his M. A. candidates to exploit the Society's materials for their theses.

Among the honors that came to him, in addition to the Society's presidency, were the following: the C. M. McClung

Award in Tennessee History (1931), the Merit Award of the American Association for State and Local History (1958), the Distinguished Alumni Award of the Millersburg Military Institute (1958), the presidency of the Southern Historical Association (1960), and honorary degrees from Washington and Lee University (Litt. D., 1949) and Knox College (LL. D., 1958).

*　*　*　*

Hesseltine, along with two other historians, was once described as an insidiously dangerous man. That was the view of Louis M. Hacker, then an associate professor of economics at Columbia University, as expressed in *Fortune Magazine* for July, 1947. Hacker began by declaring that the "only hope" for the postwar world, "beset by poverty and threatened by authoritarianism," was the "formula of liberty and equality." This formula, he said, was supported by the "great traditions of American history," properly understood.

"For this reason," Hacker continued, "it is not an academic matter that a small company of historical scholars— for the most part professors of southern birth or training now teaching in midwestern universities—should seek to undermine the great libertarian tradition of the American Civil War. Following the lead of Professors J. G. Randall, Avery O. Craven, and W. B. Hesseltine (respectively of the Universities of Illinois, Chicago, and Wisconsin), they try to demonstrate that the Civil War—which gave birth to American industrial capitalism—was a tragic mistake."

These scholars, Hacker went on to say, also misrepresented Abraham Lincoln as both an "anti-Hamiltonian" and an "anti-equalitarian," as one who had been "willing to accept the existence of the slave South." And they were unsympathetic with the Radical Republicans. But the Radical Republicans, according to Hacker, were "equalitarians and economic nationalists" who made possible the rise of the United States as a great industrial power, and Lincoln was in basic agreement with them. Lincoln and the Radicals were the keepers of a tradition which must continue to be maintained in order that "America's survival in an increasingly authoritarian world" might be assured. So the three historians were not only teaching what was objectively false. They also, apparently, were corrupting Midwestern youth with some kind of Southern taint and, in doing so, were "embarking upon a dangerous course."

As applied to Hesseltine, these criticisms went wide of the mark. True enough, he approached history with a point of view that bore the influence of his Virginia background— but also the influence of his Wisconsin residence. No one was more devoted than he to the traditional ideals of liberty and equality. These ideals he viewed from an essentially Southern and Midwestern country or small-town orientation. There was a strain of populism and La Follette progressivism in his thinking. Hacker, by contrast, had the outlook of an urban Northeasterner who shared more of the T. Roosevelt than the La Follette spirit. Hacker and others like him seemed as dangerous to Hesseltine as *he* did to them. Such "self-proclaimed liberals," he feared, were betraying the very freedoms they professed to defend. As he saw it, there was more than a trace of totalitarianism in their philosophy, since they advocated the use of federal power with scarcely any restraints.

The political convictions of Hesseltine in mid-career were set down in his book *The Rise and Fall of Third Parties,* which came out in 1948, the year after the Hacker critique. Based on a series of articles he had written for *The Progres-*

sive, the book contained not only an interpretation of third parties in the past but also a program for liberals and progressives in the future.

"The basic core of American liberal dogma—of which many self-proclaimed liberals need to be reminded—contains at least four concepts which must lie at the foundation of any progressive program," Hesseltine declared. "All four are deeply rooted in the American heritage, and the alleged liberal who rejects any of them is faithless to the progressive cause he purports to represent." The first of the four principles was "a deep-seated opposition to doctrines of the police state," and this meant "opposition to militarism, to the increase of the standing army, and unalterable opposition to conscription." The second was "devotion to democracy and to democratic procedures" in economic as well as political institutions. The third was "the injection of a sense of public responsibility into co-operatives, labor unions, and aggregations of capital," none of which should be exempt from criticism by liberals. And the fourth was "a rigid insistence on complete civil liberty for every shade of opinion and for all shades of skin."

Hesseltine added that a truly liberal-progressive program must also be based on careful planning and that this planning, in turn, must be grounded upon research and regionalism. "Socialists, and many other doctrinaires, have talked much of a 'planned society,' but, for the most part, their 'plans' have consisted in rhetorical advocacy of theoretical blueprints for a better world." Planning ought to proceed not from a "preconceived ideology" but from a "scholarly and scientific examination of the facts of society," and the whole enterprise ought to be carried forward by private groups as well as by government. It ought also to take regional differences into account. "Progressives from the Middle West and liberals of the urban East could overcome the philosophical obstacles" to co-operation between them by "recognizing that American problems differ from region to region and that one region's meat may be another region's poison."

Hesseltine followed these principles fairly consistently in the stands he took upon specific issues of his time. For instance, he gave critical support to the New Deal and was particularly enthusiastic about the Tennessee Valley Authority program as an example of democratic regional planning. During the Spanish Civil War he backed the Loyalist side; he once appeared on the platform with a group of anti-Franco priests from Spain to introduce them to a Madison audience. He opposed the Franklin D. Roosevelt policies, 1937–1941, of increasing involvement in World War II, and after the involvement became complete he joined the "peace now" movement. He also opposed the "get tough" policy of the Truman administration, but he had nothing good to say about the presidential candidacy of Henry A. Wallace, whom he dismissed as a "sorehead" and a Communist tool. In later years he grew more and more frustrated and embittered by what seemed to him the militaristic and totalitarian trend of the federal government.

With Hesseltine, as with all historians, there was undoubtedly some relationship between his concern for the future and his interpretation of the past. It does not necessarily follow, however, that his contemporary interests always determined his historical views. The relationship may often have been the other way around: the lessons he drew from historical study affected his judgment of the events of his own time. In any case, his opinions on current events were generally quite different from those of the two historians with whom he has been bracketed: Craven and Randall. Neither Craven nor Randall—the latter a great admirer of Woodrow Wilson and of Wilson's "collective

security" ideas—shared Hesseltine's strong "isolationist"
convictions, for example. Yet Hesseltine took much the
same general view of nineteenth-century American history
as did the other two. That is, he was a "revisionist" who (as
Hacker rightly charged) questioned the necessity of the
Civil War, the virtue of Radical Republicanism, and the
unmixed egalitarianism of Abraham Lincoln. Still, it is hard
to pigeonhole his ideas about history. Something of a
maverick, he at times disregarded and at other times revised
the supposed tenets of Civil War "revisionism."

Through his originality he added to historical knowledge
at a number of points. His biography of Lyman C. Draper,
as Solon J. Buck observed in a review, made "a real contribution to our understanding of the evolution of cultural
activities in the nineteenth-century Middle West." Perhaps
his most distinctive contributions, however, lay in his writings on the dynamics of regionalism, the role of Lincoln in
the Civil War, and the ending of Radical Reconstruction.

The Frederick Jackson Turner theory of the frontier and
sections had been criticized for neglecting classes and class
conflict. Hesseltine undertook to combine the influences of
both section (or region) and class in a new synthesis. He saw
the class struggle as taking place largely within particular
geographical areas of the country. Each area came to be
dominated by an emerging elite. "But in each region the
dominant group has been constantly challenged by subordinate groups who have sought to wrest the control of press
and public office, of church and school, of natural resources
and economic vantage points from the dominant group," he
explained (in the *Journal of Southern History* for February,
1960). "The competition between groups for the control of
their regions has furnished the dynamics of American history." It has also furnished the dynamics of sectionalism,
according to what Hesseltine stated or implied on various

occasions. For example, the rulers of one section might seek to maintain their position by arousing hostility against the people of another section, thus deflecting to the outside the class antagonisms that had arisen at home.

Hesseltine's essay "Some New Aspects of the Proslavery Argument" (reprinted in the present volume) illustrates the process by which class antagonism could be converted into sectional hostility. The prevalent view had been that the Southern defense of slavery was provoked by the Northern attack upon it. In his essay, however, Hesseltine indicated that the proslavery argument was largely the slaveholders' response to threats from Southern slaveless farmers, not merely a response to threats from Northern abolitionists. To maintain their position in the South, leaders of the dominant group had to discover and repel real or imaginary dangers from the North. In classroom lectures, Hesseltine elaborated upon the theme of the essay and pointed to three sources of danger, all of them appearing in 1831, a year which therefore marked a turning point in the development of proslavery propaganda. One danger came from Yankee abolitionists and was seen in the appearance of the first number of William Lloyd Garrison's fiery weekly, *The Liberator*. A second arose from the slaves themselves, as was shown by the Nat Turner insurrection in Virginia. The third was to be found among nonslaveholding Southern whites, such as those who in the Virginia legislature resumed earlier demands for the elimination of slavery in the state. With reference to Hesseltine's published essay, a more recent student of the subject, Ralph E. Morrow, has said (in the *Mississippi Valley Historical Review* for June, 1961): "This hypothesis helps to explain some peculiar features of the proslavery crusade." Morrow adds still a fourth danger and a fourth group to which the proslavery argument was directed: the guilt feelings of many slave-

owners themselves, which had to be assuaged if slavery was
to be made secure in the South.

The Civil War, Hesseltine often said, was not a "war between the states" but a "war against the states," Northern as
well as Southern. It was a war the states lost, for at the end
of it they were dominated as never before by the national
government, whose powers had grown tremendously during
the years 1861–1865.

> In personal and political terms the struggle between
> states' rights and nationalism involved a conflict between
> Abraham Lincoln, President of the United States, and the
> ill-assorted governors of twenty-five Northern and border
> states. In the beginning the governors possessed power
> as commanders-in-chief of the states' military forces, and
> had prestige by virtue of their leadership of the dominant
> political party in their respective states. In the early part
> of the war they used both power and prestige to force
> Lincoln's hand and to drive the President to accept their
> policies. But the shrewd prairie lawyer was more than a
> match for the governors. Slowly, with many a skillful
> maneuver and many a clash of personalities, the President
> proved that he alone could direct the war and that only
> he could win elections. In the end Abraham Lincoln had
> control of the Republican Party—the political instru-
> ment in nationalization—and of the military force that
> made the nation.

Such, in Hesseltine's words, is the theme of his *Lincoln and
the War Governors* (1948). In coming to this conclusion, he
no doubt exaggerated the personal role of Lincoln and the
influence of party politics, while ignoring economic and
other nationalizing trends. Nevertheless, he presented a
fresh and essentially valid interpretation of an important
aspect of the war.

In *Lincoln's Plan of Reconstruction* (1960) he repeated
the theme of Lincoln's nationalizing role and came to some

original conclusions about his Reconstruction efforts. Previous writers on the subject had concentrated very largely on Lincoln's "ten per cent plan" and had assumed that this plan would have been highly successful if Lincoln had lived to carry it out. Hesseltine, taking Reconstruction as "the basic issue of the Civil War," showed that Lincoln actually attempted a variety of approaches to it, and Hesseltine maintained that all of them ended in failure, leaving Lincoln without a workable plan at the time of his death. The basic reason for his frustration, according to Hesseltine, was the opposition of the Radical Republicans, who demanded a thorough economic and social remaking of the Southern states, while Lincoln confined himself mainly to bringing about their mere political restoration. If he failed to reconstruct those states, he nevertheless succeeded in "reconstructing" the states as a whole. He converted the old Federal Union into a new consolidated nation.

Hesseltine, in his treatment af Radical Reconstruction, has been labeled as a follower of the William A. Dunning tradition and also as a member of the Charles A. Beard and Howard K. Beale school. He did share some of Beard's and Beale's as well as Dunning's assumptions, but he also pursued independent lines of inquiry. Indeed, he did much to start the revision of the "Beard-Beale thesis," the view that Republican politicians in promoting Radical Reconstruction were responding to Northern business interests. In a 1935 article, "Economic Factors in the Abandonment of Reconstruction" (reprinted in the present volume), he demonstrated that Republican politicians and Northern businessmen came to differ regarding policy toward the South. The politicians, he explained, continued to favor the congressional program as a means of maintaining themselves in power, even after businessmen had begun to oppose it on the grounds that it produced disorder in the South and

hence discouraged business there. By 1870, businessmen
"who preferred the economic to the political exploitation
of the South" were coming to believe that their own interests might best be served by allowing the local Democrats or
Conservatives to recover control of the Southern states. Approaching the matter by way of Southern rather than
Northern interests, C. Vann Woodward elaborated on the
theme of economic factors in the abandonment of Reconstruction in his important work *Reunion and Reaction*
(1951), concluding that Reconstruction was finally given up
when representatives of Northern business and Southern
property came to an understanding. Other historians,
notably Robert F. Sharkey and Stanley Coben, later advanced beyond Hesseltine's conception of differences between Republican politicians and businessmen by indicat-
ing that there were also differences among the businessmen
themselves on such questions as the tariff, the currency, and
the Reconstruction program.

Hesseltine also anticipated one of Woodward's conclusions when, in *Ulysses S. Grant, Politician* (1935), he said
with regard to the disputed election of 1876: "Republicans
surrendered the Negro to the Southern ruling class, and
abandoned the idealism of Reconstruction, in return for
the peaceable inauguration of their President." A reviewer
(Elbert J. Benton) picked out this sentence to dissent from
it: "That is surely not a sound historical interpretation of
the Wormley Hotel conference." Indeed, Hesseltine had
merely tossed off the statement as an aside, without having
gone deeply into the settlement of 1877, which was only
tangential to his main subject. But Woodward, after exhaustive research (which led him to dismiss the Wormley
Hotel conference as relatively unimportant), came to essentially the same conclusion in *Reunion and Reaction* as

Hesseltine had suggested earlier in one of his incidental remarks.

Such obiter dicta provided much of the strength—and much of the weakness—in Hesseltine's writings. Reviewers praised him, on the one hand, for "rare insight," for "forceful arguments" and "pungent judgments," for "historical criticism of a high order," for "an artistic blend of fact and interpretation," and for "a hand skillful in preserving human interest." Reviewers criticized him, on the other hand, for "oversimplification," for "sweeping generalization," and for "language too extreme to be taken seriously." But even the adverse critics, those who thought he sometimes went beyond his sources, generally agreed that the work in question had at least the merit of intellectual stimulation: it would, as a typical reviewer said, "provoke thought." This ability to arouse interest, to generalize brilliantly if at times erratically, to open new vistas for possible exploration—this was perhaps the greatest virtue of Hesseltine the history writer, as it also was of Hesseltine the history teacher.

*   *   *   *

The essays chosen for this memorial volume include some of the more significant of Hesseltine's shorter pieces. The editor's aim, however, has not necessarily been to assemble "the best" but rather to provide a sampling that would illustrate the range of the author's subjects and treatments over most of his career. Another editor might have made a somewhat different selection. The articles are reprinted here in the form in which they originally appeared, except for the following kinds of emendations: (1) changes in capitalization, with a view to consistency, since the various journals from which the articles are taken had different policies in this regard; (2) minor changes in punctuation and in wording, with a view to clarity or felicity of style, in a few instances where it seemed that the author himself, had he been overseeing the republication of the essays, would have made or approved the alterations.

The bibliography is intended to list all of Hesseltine's books and articles, including those of which he was joint author. It does not, however, list all of his book reviews, which seemed much too numerous for a full and accurate record here. The roster of his doctoral candidates is included because of a conviction that he valued his students at least as much as his publications.

RICHARD N. CURRENT

Greensboro, North Carolina
February, 1968

Contents

ONE

Look Away, Dixie!

SINCE the days of the Civil War, and even before that direful conflict, the denizens of the erstwhile Confederacy have been particularly prone to praise and exalt the Southern way of life. Cheap novelists, visionless rhymesters, motion picture intellectuals, and writers of advertisements have seized upon the broad verandas of the mythical manor houses of the Old South and burst into rapturous paeans of praise for a civilization which never existed. Such people, confusing the pseudo-aristocrats of the Old South with the landed gentry of England, and endowing them with unpossessed and undreamed virtues, have done a real harm to the South. They have served to create in the minds of Southern people a false concept of the social order, and they have made the South appear rather ridiculous to the rest of the country. Southern people, remembering the novels and the movies, have attempted, by adopting eccentricities which the novelists have said were characteristic, to live up to the expectations of outsiders. There are even said to be "professional" Southerners who stand at atten-

A review of *I'll Take My Stand: The South and the Agrarian Tradition*. By TWELVE SOUTHERNERS. (New York, Harper's, 1930.) Reprinted by permission from the *Sewanee Review*, 39: 97–103 (January–March, 1931).

tion while the band plays "Dixie" and interlard their conversation with references to "befo de wah."

The real South, which existed before the war and has par-
tially continued down to the present time, was quite a different thing from this sentimentalized caricature. There was
a South, a South that still exists in places, with distinctive
characteristics and a mode and method of life essentially
different from that of the rest of the country. It was a land
of simple people, with simple arts and leisurely graces, with
pride of family, and a love of kin, and withal a gracious, almost lazy, carelessness for the economic standards of the
businesslike North. It is this South which the authors of
this book [*I'll Take My Stand*] seek to present and to preserve; and if they but succeed in convincing the Southern
people that the old South was not a land of broad verandas
which stunk of lavender and old lace, they will have rendered a real service.

The South which actually existed, in that time now made
roseate by distance, was a community based upon an agricultural economy and living close to the soil. Its vaunted
aristocracy, with the possible exception of a few old and
wealthy families of the tidewater, was a "squirearchy"—the
product of frontier conditions and definitely "on the make."
Moreover, but a small group of the Southern people were
even of the "squirearchy." The real tone and color of society in the old South was given by the yeoman farmer,
owner of a few acres, possessor of a few slaves, and master
of his own destiny. Though the squires held the political
offices, and occasionally forgot his interests in seeking their
own and though novelists and mythmakers have neglected
him, the yeoman farmer was the dominant factor in the old
South. He it was who objected to abolitionism, he who
profited from the doctrine of states' rights, he who voted

the Democratic ticket, and finally it was he who fought, bled, and died in the armies of the Confederacy.

Although the contributors to this symposium spend but little space in defining the social system which the yeoman farmer produced, they are on solid ground when they ignore the lavender-and-old-lace tradition, and deal with this hitherto unknown South. The stand which they are taking in this book with its song-borrowed title is that the South of the yeoman farmer, with all of the fine culture which they attribute to it, is being threatened by the southward march of the industrial revolution. In broad terms, the South faces the problem of succumbing to the machine age or making a definite effort to preserve the agrarian way of life. Herein twelve Southerners, already yclept "The Young Confederates," take their stand against industrialization.

Opposition to the age of the machine, with its emphasis on production, its lack of consideration for human beings and its crushing effects on individualism, is not particularly new. Beginning with the Luddite riots and continuing to this present volume, there has been a mighty army of philosophers, poets, laborers, and reactionaries marching in the crusade against the mechanical devices of the modern age. As far as their diatribes against industrialism are concerned, these Young Confederates have nothing to say which has not been better said many times before.

But if there is nothing new in their antipathy to industrialism, these young intellectuals are certainly making a startling contribution in offering the social system of the yeoman South as a substitute for the machine age. Fearful lest machinery displace the leisure of the South, the Young Confederates, in the most humorless series of essays that has been published for many a day, take up the cudgels in defense of the agrarian tradition.

John Crowe Ransom, professor of English, poet, and re-
cent author of "God Without Thunder," throws the open-
ing spitball against the machine age. Opposing the flux and
instability of modern life, he condemns the twin doctrines
of progress and service and praises the Old South as a place
where there was stability and "establishment." "The establishment had a sufficient economic base; it was meant to be
stable rather than provisional; it had got beyond the pio-
neering stage; it provided leisure, and its benefits were already being enjoyed." In order to regain this "establishment" the Southerner, according to Prof. Ransom, should
"arouse the sectional feeling of the South to its highest pitch
in defense of all of the old ways that are threatened," and
reanimate the Democratic party with an "agrarian, conservative, anti-industrial" program. After this interesting pair
of suggestions, Donald Davidson, also a poet and literary
editor of this book, discusses the low state of the arts in an
industrial society. True art, he asserts, is not encouraged by
art museums, and there "are more and more poems about
the difficulty of writing poetry being written." He, too, proposes deposing industrialism as the regulating god of modern society, and suggests that the provincialism of the South
be restored as the only life an artist can find congenial.

F. L. Owsley, historian, recounts the story of the struggle
of industrialism and agrarianism which culminated in the
Civil War. Unfortunately, the victory of the North in that
war resulted in spiritual as well as in material conquests,
and the professor deplores the teaching of "Northern" history to Southern children. John Gould Fletcher goes Dr.
Owsley one better and opposes teaching the children of the
South anything. An opponent of the public-school idea, he
proposes the reëstablishment of the outmoded academy with
its classical curricula as the best education for the South.
Realizing the impossibility of this proposal, he demands

that education shall be directed to training the intellectual élite, while agricultural schools and manual training institutes might care for the rest of mankind in the reconstructed South. Following this, Lyle H. Lanier criticizes the doctrine of progress, renounces the capitalist program, with its attempt to industrialize agriculture, and demands the rehabilitation of agriculture and the individualism which accompanies it. Then Allen Tate, humanist and biographer, takes the stand to announce that the South never had an articulated religion and must therefore adopt political methods to save its traditional economic system.

Also against the present economic system and in favor of the yeoman economy is H. C. Nixon, who finds stability and happiness in agricultural Denmark and depression and unemployment in industrial England. A. N. Lytle agrees with Dr. Nixon and deplores the arrival of the doctrine of progress on the farms. "A farm is not a place to grow wealthy; it is a place to grow corn," he asserts in condemning the invasion of the fields by agricultural machinery. Unfortunately for his argument against the progressive farmer, he makes the mistake of carrying his reader to view a typical farm of the class he apotheosizes. The farmer milks a cow with one hand while the other holds a pail, and then he churns until the butter "collects in small yellow clods on top" of the milk. "These clods are separated from the buttermilk and put in a bowl." After the churning, he goes to a dinner of "hot steaming vegetables, all set about the table, small hills around the mountains of meat at the ends, a heaping plate of fried chicken, a turkey, a plate of guineas, or a one-year ham, spiced, and if company is there, baked in wine. A plate of bread is at each end of the table; a bowl of chitterlings has been set at the father's elbow, and pigs' feet for those that like them." In the evening, after the work is done, there is a "play-party," where the swains and gals

play games. All of this sounds so interesting that one is almost tempted to follow the exhortation to "throw out the
radio and take down the fiddle from the wall. Forsake the
movies for the play-parties and the square dances. And turn
away from the liberal capons who fill the pulpits as preach-
ers. Seek a priesthood that may manifest the will and intelligence to renounce science and search out the Word in the
authorities." One is almost tempted—until one remembers
that one left the farm because such food was only served
when the city cousin was visiting, and that no one ever
milked a cow that way.

The other contributors to the book have little to offer in
the way of elaborating its fundamental thesis. Robert Penn
Warren believes that the Negro problem will be solved by
a return to agrarianism, and John Donald Wade breaks into
fiction to tell the story of one man who struggled against
industrialism—and died. Henry Blue Kline also goes into
fiction to present a character who sought a cultural and cul-
tured society—and found it in Nashville. Finally Stark
Young brings up the rear guard with a picture of Coolidge
as the cultureless boor who is the typical product of industrial society. And at the end he asks if "Publicity, Success,
Competition, Speed and Speedways, Progress, Donations
and Hot Water" are the end of man's living?

With many of these viewpoints, the intelligent student of
the Southern problem will find himself in sympathy. Agriculture remains the basic industry of the South, and a too
rapid transition from an agricultural to an industrial order
of society will inevitably produce a host of evils which may
well invalidate any benefits which may be derived from the
exchange. However, the Young Confederates of Nashville
make themselves a little ridiculous in apotheosizing agrarian culture and elevating the yeoman farmer to a pedestal.
Agrarian culture, as anyone reared on a farm will tell them,

is almost a contradiction in terms, and the average farmer of the South most certainly is undeserving of a pedestal. Moreover, this is not only true of the South at this present moment, but it has been true throughout the history of the section.

At no time in its history, from Jamestown to Dayton, has the American South been other than a horrible example of the spiritual failure of agrarianism. Before the Civil War its sturdy yeomanry produced no poets worthy of the name, they created no statues, and they erected no cathedrals. Their philosophers, their scholars, and their thinkers were pitifully few. Although they produced politicians and army officers in abundance, the careers of these, directed as they were into anti-social channels, are not particularly worthy of praise. Since Reconstruction, the record, although somewhat better, is still not very conclusive that the South can make a consistent contribution to the art of the world. Its spokesmen in the legislative halls have been Vardamans, Bleases, and Heflins, with just enough admixture of Wilsons and Pages to lend color to its claims to respectability. Its poets—present company excepted—have added but little to the luster of the section. Its novelists, themselves largely the products of the most industrialized sections of the South, have drawn their nourishment from New York. With but few exceptions, its universities are inferior to those of the North, and its school systems are backward and chaotic. The places where these things are not true are those places which have succumbed to the drugging influence of industrialism. Agrarian society has failed even more dismally than industrial to foster the arts, which, throughout human history, have been the products of the cities rather than the rural regions.

One other mistake which these Southerners make is their attitude toward the coming industrialism. However worth-

while their attitude of skepticism towards industrialization
might be, they are making a mistake in adopting a policy
of obscurantism. Most of them realize that the industrialization of the South is inevitable, and it would be better for
them to face that fact, and attempt to make the most of it,
rather than to adopt an ostrich trick and stick their heads
in the soil.

If the South in its industrialization is going to preserve
some of its distinctive characteristics, it must consciously
attempt to deal with the existing situation. The South has
the opportunity to regulate industry before industry gets a
strangle hold on the section. It is in a position where it can
profit from the experience of the rest of the nation in such
matters as the relations of capital and labor. It can consciously adopt a policy which will make great aggregations
of capital responsive to social needs, and endow corpora-
tions, by process of law, if need be, with a social conscience.
None of these results can be obtained by a policy of obscurantism, or by fostering a spirit of reaction. To quote one
of these Young Confederates against himself, Donald Davidson has given poetic expression to this idea in his "Sod
of the Battlefields!"

> The U. D. C.'s still meet
> Indomitably, despairing of their granddaughters.
> The Union is saved, Lee has surrendered forever.
> Today, Lorena, it is forbidden to be
> A Southerner. One is American now.

But, however much this is to be deplored, the Southerner
declares:

> This is my body and spirit,
> Broken but never tamed, risen from the bloody sod,
> Walking suddenly alive in a new morning.

The South has the opportunity to arise from the bloody sod of her past, and walk alive in the new morning, but the battle cry of that awakening can never be the reactionary "I'll Take My Stand," but must be that other phrase of the song—"Look Away! Dixie Land."

TWO

Tennessee's Invitation to Carpetbaggers

THE emphasis which has been placed upon the political history of the Reconstruction of the South has tended to elevate the political "Carpetbagger" to a position of prominence. The less dramatic, but more abiding brother of the political adventurer who came to exploit the South, the economic "Carpetbagger," has been lost from sight. Moreover, with the recovery of Conservative control in the Southern states, the carpetbagger, whether economic or political, has been made into a figure of ill repute. The more spectacular of the political adventurers doubtless deserved the odium which has been attached to the name, but even in the ranks of the political carpetbagger there were many who did not deserve wholesale condemnation. The economic carpetbagger, the man who came South, carpetbag in hand, after the war to exploit the natural resources of the land rather than the newly enfranchised freedman, de-

Read before the East Tennessee Historical Society at Knoxville on October 2, 1931. Reprinted by permission from the *East Tennessee Historical Society's Publications*, 4: 102–115 (January, 1932).

serves commendation rather than condemnation. In fact, the Radical governments of the Southern states, with the approval of the Conservatives, attempted to encourage the immigration of Northerners and Europeans to their states. South Carolina and Tennessee established immigration boards to entice immigrants, and acts were passed to subsidize agencies which would send in immigrants.[1] In Tennessee, where many of the forces of Reconstruction were more clear cut than in the other Southern states, a considerable effort was made to attract immigrants.

Like most of the South, Tennessee had been shunned by immigrants before the Civil War. The presence of slavery, and the greater attractiveness of the Western soils, combined to lead immigrants away from the South. More people left the slave states for free states than came in from the North. In this situation, east Tennessee, which was not contaminated by the presence of the peculiar institution to an oppressive extent, suffered with the rest of the state. Despite the fact that an Englishman, residing in east Tennessee, published in London a brochure calling on dairy maids, Scotch shepherds with collie dogs, hatters, and textile workers to migrate to east Tennessee,[2] the section suffered from the general neglect which the immigrant accorded the South. East Tennesseeans, as a result, adopted a defense mechanism and declared that they did not want immigrants among them. The raucous Parson Brownlow screamed to the Reverend Pryne: "Leave us in the peaceable possession of our slaves, and our Northern Neighbors may have all the

---

[1] Hermann Bokum, *The Tennessee Handbook and Immigrants Guide . . .*, 129. For full title, see note 39 *infra*.

[2] H. Gray Smith, *A Brief Historical, Statistical and Descriptive Review of East Tennessee, United States of America: Developing its immense Agricultural, Mining and Manufacturing Advantages with Remarks to Emigrants* (London, 1842), 50.

paupers and convicts that pour in upon us from European prisons!"[3] In 1850 only 178,174 out of a total free population of 763,285 in Tennessee had been born outside the state. Most of those had come from other Southern states, and only 5,740 were Europeans.[4]

By 1860, Parson Brownlow, who always reserved the right to change his mind, began to feel that capital should be encouraged to migrate to east Tennessee to develop its mineral resources.[5] The war left east Tennessee with a depleted population,[6] and when Brownlow returned from exile, he began to advocate the immigration of loyal men into his section. "We call the attention of loyal men in other states to the wants of this portion of Tennessee, and especially Knoxville. We want . . . " tin shops, house carpenters, boot and shoe shops, tanneries, tailors, blacksmiths, saddlers, harness makers, carriage makers, and Union mechanics, "to take the place of a vile set of rebel lick-spitters who have had their day, and whose prospective course, and persecution of loyal men forbid that they should ever do business here again."[7]

Brownlow's interest in immigration was political and social rather than economic. In November, 1864, he deplored the fact that Union women walked the streets of Louisville begging, while their husbands were in the Federal army. "Thanks to God," he exclaimed, "labor is everywhere remunerative, and when this war is over the scornful, proud, and bitter rebel woman will find herself upon a level with

---

[3] J. F. Rhodes, *History of the United States from the Compromise of 1850*, I, 355. Cf. William G. Brownlow and Abraham Pryne, *Ought American Slavery be Perpetuated?* (Philadelphia, 1858).

[4] *Compendium of the U. S. Census for 1850*, 116–117.

[5] *Parson Brownlow's Book*, 213–214.

[6] T. W. Humes, *Loyal Mountaineers of Tennessee*, 302.

[7] *Brownlow's Knoxville Whig and Rebel Ventilator*, Jan. 16, 1864.

the poor Union woman, without a gang of negroes at her
command. . . . We hope to see the day in east Tennessee
when it will no longer be dishonorable for young ladies to
learn to *sew* and work in the kitchen. Nay, we desire to see
the day come when the honest and virtuous poor, who have
been punished and persecuted by the hateful aristocracy,
will be called upon, in mercy, to give their descendants em-
ployment."[8] The abolition of slavery was, to Brownlow, a
means of bringing about the millennium.

Colonel Nat G. Taylor, a leading Unionist, was also convinced that the end of slavery would save the state, and informed the Parson, just before he became governor, that
the ratification of the Thirteenth Amendment would cause
an increase of three-quarters of a million in the population
of the state, and with Negroes free, the development of the
great natural resources of the state would begin.[9] In his in-
augural address, Brownlow, elaborating on this theme, declared that slavery was a "nuisance" which had obstructed
the development of the state. "One of the signs of the times,"
he continued, "is that the natural features of the Southern
States are now being expatiated upon, in order that enter-
prising emigrants may be led to come among us, and add to
our capital and enterprise. Tennessee holds out inducements to wealthy and industrious emigrants that no other
border state affords."[10] But it is evident that Brownlow
was more interested in the influx of capital than of labor,
for, in his message to the legislature, he pointed out that
there was reason to expect an increase of population after
the war, and, enumerating the state debt, he suggested an
increase of taxes.[11]

---

[8] *Ibid.,* Nov. 16, 1864.
[9] Taylor to Brownlow, *ibid.,* Feb. 22, 1865.
[10] *Whig and Ventilator,* April 12, 1865.
[11] *Ibid.,* April 19, 1865.

The expected influx of capital to the South occurred. Cotton was high, and the Southern planters were eager for capital. Desirous of selling their lands, the planters welcomed the Northerner who came south with the idea that the Negro would work for him out of gratitude. All over the Black Belt, cotton plantations were sold or leased to ex-officers of the Union armies.[12] Newspapers in Tennessee urged their readers who had lands, mill or factory sites, or coal, copper, or lead mines, to advertise. The papers assured their readers that the notices would come to the attention of merchants, manufacturers, and bankers—"the very class of men . . . whose help is needed in developing the wealth of our great state."[13] Companies were formed to develop the natural resources of the state. In 1865 the Tennessee Colonial, Agricultural, Mining, and Manufacturing Company, composed of one Tennesseean and four New Yorkers, was chartered with a capital of $200,000, and authorized to raise vineyards and engage in mining and manufacturing.[14] The next year, the Tennessee Colonial and Immigration Company was formed.[15] The companies were evidently intent on selling land to adventurous Yankees, but they do not seem to have accomplished much. In 1865 the state senate created a committee on immigration, which made no report.[16] In the early part of 1867 the legislature incorporated, with a capital of five million dollars, the American Emigration Society, which was designed to sell land to northern and foreign immigrants.[17]

To some extent, these efforts to attract capital to Ten-

---

[12] W. L. Fleming, *Civil War and Reconstruction in Alabama*, 322–3.

[13] Nashville *Daily Press and Times*, Jan. 1, 1867.

[14] *Acts of Tennessee*, 1st session, 34th General Assembly, 74.

[15] *Ibid.*, 2nd session, 311.

[16] *Ibid.*, 411.

[17] *Ibid.*, 119–21.

nessee were successful. General J. T. Wilder, of Indiana, who had fought at Chattanooga and Knoxville, returned to Tennessee after the war, and began the manufacture of iron in Roane County.[18] Iron foundries were opened by Northern capital in Chattanooga,[19] and the city directories of Chattanooga and Knoxville show a tremendous influx of Northern business. In 1869 Northern immigrants owned one-sixth of the property in Knoxville.[20]

But if Northern capital came to the South, Northern labor did not. The Conservative press was as eager as the Radicals to obtain laborers. The Negroes were disorganized and were refusing to work, and the planters had hopes that Northern and foreign labor would be steadier. "Immigration Societies," mostly fraudulent, were formed to furnish labor to the planters,[21] and in west Tennessee the planters perceived in immigration a means not only of restoring prosperity to agriculture, but of restoring the conservatives to power. The theory was advanced that Tennessee needed "a regular system of labor, and it can be obtained only by importation from abroad." Ignorant Germans and Irish, moreover, would vote as the planters directed. But the Radical press pointed out that foreign immigrants who entered Missouri and the northwest "all vote the Republican ticket as faithfully as they hew wood and draw water."[22]

The realization of the fact that the immigrants were supporters of the Radical regime did not, in general, incline the Conservatives to favor the newcomers. Despite the fact that the Conservatives assured the immigrants that they were welcome, the Radicals played up occasional outrages

---

[18] *Facts and Figures . . . Concerning East Tennessee,* 24.
[19] Chattanooga *News,* April 9, 1930.
[20] *Brownlow's Knoxville Whig and Ventilator,* May 5, 1869.
[21] Fleming, *Civil War and Reconstruction in Alabama,* 318, 718.
[22] Nashville *Daily Press and Times,* Feb. 13, 1867.

against them in order to keep them loyal to the Republican control. "Shoot and stab Union farmers, and burn down their sawmills," exhorted the Radical press when a Northerner's sawmill was burned; "It proves that rebels are anxious to encourage Northern immigrants, and saves the trouble of proving one's loyalty by a test oath."[23] Such exhortations merely served to increase the resentment of the Conservatives.

Whatever immigration of labor there was into Tennessee went into the eastern section. East Tennessee, loyalist and Republican, was the most orderly part of the state. The exodus of "a few men who made themselves obnoxious by their oppression of Union men during the war" and "sought more congenial society elsewhere" made room for "hundreds of families" of loyal men.[24] Of 367 immigrants who passed through Columbus, Ohio, in February 1867, 139 were going to Missouri and 35 to Tennessee. Since Missouri was also Republican, Radicals in Tennessee, pointing out that Tennessee's immigration had increased since the passage of her Radical laws, declared: "The people admire the radical policy."[25] West Tennessee received no immigrants because of its "ruffianism," while east Tennessee boasted of the arrival of from six to eight families a week.[26] "There is a large number of farmers in Tennessee," declared the Radical organ in Nashville, "who are pressed for money, and would gladly sell a part of their lands, but no immigration comes to relieve them. Immigrants prefer lands of the strongly loyal portion of the state to the richest lands of this division, where there is a bitter opposition to the State Government. It is a remarkable fact that Missouri and East Ten-

---

23 *Ibid.*, Feb. 21, 1867.
24 *Ibid.*, Jan. 15, 1867.
25 *Ibid.*, Feb. 28, 1867.
26 *Ibid.*, March 19, 1867.

nessee are receiving more new settlers than all the rest of the South. Immigrants want peace, and they naturally seek that in loyal communities."[27]

Possibly because of the unsettled condition of the state, most of the immigrants came in groups of several families, or even in colonies. In the summer of 1867 a colony of Pennsylvanians purchased some 40,000 acres of iron lands in Hickman County and proposed to manufacture iron. This colony was welcomed by the press of the state, and farmers with surplus lands were urged to offer small farms for sale to such immigrants. The colony was hailed as the "harbinger of better days" for the South.[28] At Sneedsville, a colony of thirty families of "thrifty and independent" Pennsylvanians was settled.[29] Lands in the South were selling at the time as cheap as five dollars an acre, and it was suggested that companies be organized in the North to buy up Southern lands and settle them with German, Norwegian, or Dutch farmers. "No investment offers so sure and large a profit."[30]

The desire for European immigrants even led the farmers of Maury County to contribute to the building of a Catholic church in Columbia, in hopes that Irish would be attracted to the community.[31] The various German societies in Nashville called a meeting of all German citizens at Turner Hall "to take into consideration the best measures for promoting German immigration to this state." Simultaneous meetings were held in Chattanooga, Knoxville, and Memphis, and it was hoped that branch societies would be formed throughout the state. These societies would assist

---

[27] *Ibid.,* April 29, 1867.
[28] *Ibid.,* April 22 and Sept. 11, 1867.
[29] *Ibid.,* Feb. 14, 1868.
[30] *Ibid.,* Feb. 5, 1868.
[31] *Ibid.,* Aug. 31, 1867.

immigrants to find suitable locations, and help them get established.[32] The "German Association of the City of Nashville" was established, and received a charter from the legislature. By the act of incorporation, the society was "authorized to procure laborers for parties applying to them; to act as agents for land owners desirous of selling their property, and for parties wishing to buy lands in the State of Tennessee."[33] The society held regular meetings for a time. At its first meeting, it suggested that the state establish a bureau of immigration.[34]

When the legislators met in the fall of 1867, Governor Brownlow informed them that his "fond hope . . . that a tide of immigration would set in to this State from the Northern States and from Europe" had not been gratified. That the "mild and healthy climate, fertile soil, magnificent scenery, and pure and abundant water" of Tennessee had not enticed "men of capital and enterprise," he attributed to the "intolerant and proscriptive spirit" of the former Confederates. This spirit, said the governor, was the obvious result of the "insane" policy of President Johnson, "who constantly holds out . . . [to these pestilential disloyalists] . . . the prospect of being restored to power at an early day." But as the influence of Johnson was declining, Brownlow hoped for a better spirit in the state, and suggested that the legislature take steps to encourage immigration.[35] Both Senate and House appointed standing committees on immigration,[36] and in December, 1867, the state board of immigration of five members was established.

---

[32] *Ibid.,* Aug. 14, 1867.

[33] *Acts of Tennessee,* 1st session, 35th General Assembly, 24.

[34] Nashville *Daily Press and Times,* Aug. 21, 1867.

[35] *Acts of Tennessee,* 1st session, 35th General Assembly, Appendix, 15–16.

[36] *Acts of Tennessee,* 1st session, 35th Assembly, 303, 317.

The state board of immigration was authorized to "do all and everything which may and will advance and encourage immigration." It might publish books and pamphlets, and advertise in Northern newspapers. Agents were to be sent to Northern and Eastern states. One thousand dollars were appropriated to carry on this work, and the board was allowed to receive contributions from any who might be interested.[37] As commissioner under the board, Brownlow appointed the Reverend Hermann Bokum, formerly an agent of the Freedman's Bureau in east Tennessee, and described as a "ripe German scholar." During the war, Bokum had been in the immigration bureau of the department of state in Washington.[38]

Less than three months after his appointment, Bokum published a book setting forth the attractions of Tennessee. After a description of the state as a whole, Bokum dealt with the counties of each division. The thirty counties of east Tennessee were described in detail in forty-nine pages, whereas forty-two pages sufficed for the fifty-four counties of the other two divisions. In the general account of the state, east Tennessee was most frequently referred to, and generally to the disparagement of the other sections. West

---

[37] *Ibid.*, 11–12 (December 4, 1867).

[38] Knoxville *Daily Free Press*, Dec. 17, 1867; Bokum, *op. cit.*, 3–4, 126 note. The state comptroller in his report to the legislature believed that this state effort would bring results. "If cheap lands, a fertile soil, a most salubrious and invigorating atmosphere, a home market for all the products of the soil, are the considerations that influence immigrants in their choice of future homes, then surely Tennessee offers them all, with fewer drawbacks than does any other state in the Union. . . . Hitherto, the existence of slavery repelled from our state, that class of immigrants best calculated to develop our agricultural wealth. Now that this objection is removed, and that the large landed proprietors find it to their interest to cut up their estates, and sell, or lease, in such quantity as may be desired, we have every confidence that the tide of immigration will soon set Tennessee-ward." *Reports* to the 35th General Assembly, 55.

Tennessee received only fourteen pages, and most of them dealt with the city of Memphis where there were twelve thousand Germans.

The animus back of this preference for east Tennessee was obviously political. The war, declared Bokum, had swept away the institution of slavery, and afforded an opportunity for East Tennesseeans and Northerners to get acquainted. "And it gradually placed the people of East Tennessee, in consequence of their unbending loyalty, in a position of great influence in the direction of the affairs of the state." This position had been used to reestablish the state's finances, restore order, establish public schools, and develop the resources of the state. The agricultural resources were dealt with, but Bokum showed a greater enthusiasm in writing about the mineral resources and the industrial opportunities. The presence of slavery had hitherto prevented the working of the mineral resources, but Bokum anticipated a great stimulus in that field. As for manufactures, the people of east Tennessee were earnestly advocating their establishment. "They have come to the conclusion," he asserted, "that they are too poor to do without manufactories," and were realizing that an overemphasis on agriculture was making them "poorer every day." The legislature had declared that, without industrial development, Tennessee would never be other than a pauper state.

As for agriculture, which received but little attention from the scholarly German, Bokum promised a renaissance when the growing of cotton, which had supported the slave system, and which had exhausted the soil, should give way before diversified crops. West Tennessee, thought Bokum, might in time rival Illinois as a cereal producing section, and the introduction of a farming population that had been accustomed to a better system of agriculture might be a help. "Still it ought to be borne in mind," said he, bearing in mind the minerals, "that they can only aid in the work which is to be accomplished."

Since Bokum was more interested in the migration of capital than of labor, he found himself forced to dispel the illusion that lawlessness prevailed in the state. He offered his own testimony that there was not a more law-abiding section of the country than east Tennessee, and declared that capitalists had invested heavily in the section and were extending their operations. Moreover, he argued, "the great mass of the citizens of Tennessee are favorable to immigration, and are likely to treat the immigrant with courtesy and kindness. In this respect differences of political opinion have but little weight. . . . I have found that gentlemen who hold political opinions diagonally opposite the one from the other are still ready to join with each other in building up the State by introducing into it capital and an industrious immigrant population."

In an address to the people, Bokum appealed for support for the state board of immigration and urged the legislature to send agents to Northern cities and to Europe to set forth Tennessee's advantages. Farmers with lands for sale should unite in advertising them in newspapers and circulars, and he suggested that in each county there should be established associations which would co-operate with the state board in disseminating information. Several such associations were formed, and the legislature, in order to encourage the project, purchased two thousand dollars worth of Bokum's book for circulation.[39]

---

[39] Hermann Bokum, *The Tennessee Handbook and Immigrants Guide: Giving a Description of the State of Tennessee; Its Agricultural and Mineralogical Character; Its Waterpower, Timber, Soil, and Climate; Its Various Railroad Lines, Completed in Progress, and Projected; Its Adaptation for Stock Raising, Grape Culture, etc.,*

The publication of this book had considerable effect in creating interest within Tennessee, and doubtless some were attracted from the outside. A bill was introduced into the legislature to invite capital and manufacturing, and it was proposed to form an association to encourage industry. During 1868 a number of colonies were established in the state, possibly as a result of this official effort. A colony of one hundred from Pennsylvania and Indiana was established on a tract of land purchased for the purpose in Overton county; English grape growers established themselves in Grundy county. In Cumberland county, the efforts of W. W. Powell, the land agent, resulted in 119 immigrants coming in, and in Roane county, General Wilder's iron establishment was successful, and had a town of three hundred around it. An immigration company was planned in Memphis which would settle European colonies along the Mississippi and

---

etc., With Special Reference to the Subject of Immigration (Philadelphia, 1868). See especially pp. 6–7, 13, 54, 84, 95, 101–2, 105–6, 109, 132–35. A sample of some of the information which was thought to have an appeal for immigrants is the following letter from W. W. Powell of Cumberland County to Bokum: "My first knowledge of this country dates back to May, 1860, at which time I came here a confirmed invalid, made so by bronchitis, affection of the kidneys, chronic rheumatism, liver complaint, jaundice, and general debility. From all these difficulties I was in a few months entirely relieved, with the single exception of bronchitis from which I was so far relieved as to be entirely exempt, up to the present time, from suffering. My residence here during the entire summer of 1860 secured to me a degree of health and strength never before enjoyed, and which I have in no measure lost. I have now, at the age of sixty-two, the elasticity of boyhood, and the firm step and ruddy complexion of sound health. Under these circumstances you will not be surprised at my unqualified testimony in favor of this climate. I have carefully watched its influence upon the condition of others, as well as my own, and have often questioned what disease it, in connection with a free and persistent use of our chalybee waters, will not cure, or at least greatly alleviate" (p. 101).

Tennessee railroads.[40] Brownlow received letters, even from Iowa, asking for more information about the state.[41]

Not all of these "plantations" were successful: a "Dutch" colony near Columbia failed, and the local press declared that the Germans were no better than Negroes, who at least were able to speak English.[42] Moreover, the report persisted that Tennesseeans warred on strangers from the North. The Nashville organ of the Radicals, in denying this, declared: "We would rejoice heartily to see a hundred thousand Northern business men settle in this state during the present year. Between this class of newcomers and old residents we make no distinction." However, the paper declared that the "riffraff" who came in for politics were not wanted.[43] An Ohioan at Greeneville wrote north that east Tennessee, at least, welcomed immigrants and that the "Southern Feeling" was gone from all but the minds of a few "fossils."

On the whole, immigrants seem to have been desired by all social and political classes. The annual report of the secretary of the interior for 1867 showed that immigration to the United States was on the increase, and estimated that every immigrant added one thousand dollars annually to the productive wealth of the country. Since this made the laborer as desirable as the capitalist, Bokum was exhorted to "take courage, and work with spirit, hope and renewed vigor."[44]

---

[40] Nashville *Daily Press and Times,* Feb. 21, March 2, April 6, Sept. 21, March 23, 1868.

[41] *Whig and Ventilator,* March 18, 1868.

[42] *Press and Times,* April 1, 1868.

[43] *Ibid.,* July 15, 1868.

[44] *Whig and Ventilator,* March 18; *Press and Times,* March 9, 1868.

Bokum did not need to be exhorted to work. In March, 1868, he reported that he had received detailed accounts of their resources from several counties, and that large numbers of Northern people had entered the state. One speech before a farmers club in New York had resulted in fifty letters of inquiry, and many people were moving. Cumberland, Warren, Coffee, Franklin, Dickson, and Bradley counties had received accessions through his efforts.[45] In May he moved his headquarters to New York and had received fifty dollars in subscriptions to aid his work. One man offered to be one of one hundred to give one hundred dollars each, if the state would appropriate $10,000 to encourage immigration.[46] Bokum spent much of his time writing letters to New York papers, assuring them of the law-abiding tendencies of east Tennessee, and pointing out the investment of Northern capital in the copper mines at Ducktown, in the zinc mines of Mossy Creek, the iron foundries in Greene county, and the marble quarries in Hawkins as proof of the reign of law and order. The presence of a snow storm in May was used by Bokum to praise the climate of Tennessee; two months before, when New York was in the midst of such a storm, Bokum had stood on the top of Lookout Mountain, "intensely enjoying the invigorating and exhilirating air."[47] Speeches were also used by Bokum to set forth Tennessee's attractions.[48] Moreover, Bokum traveled over Tennessee, inspecting colonies, new industries, and the resources of the counties.[49]

Despite these activities, Brownlow was not satisfied.

---

[45] *Press and Times,* March 14, 1868.

[46] *Ibid.,* May 16, 1868.

[47] Bokum to the New York *Tribune,* quoted in *Whig and Ventilator,* May 20, 1868.

[48] *Whig and Ventilator,* June 10 (speech at Pittsburgh).

[49] See letters from Bokum in the *Press and Times,* Aug. 14 and 29, 1868.

When the legislature met in the fall of 1868, the governor stated that his convictions on immigration had grown stronger, even though Tennessee was being avoided by immigrants. The many advantages of the state—climate, soils, forests, minerals, railroads, and scenery—which were so obvious to Brownlow, were not appreciated by the immigrant, and the governor decided that further steps should be taken. He suggested the incorporation of a state immigration society, and the appropriation of an annual sum to encourage immigration. Other Southern states had adopted this method, and Brownlow believed that the future held out hopes for the South. This optimism was inspired by the recent election. "The election of Grant and Colfax means peace," he asserted; "it means that carpetbaggers are not to be molested in Tennessee; that capital, coming to us from abroad, whether of brains or hands, or money, is not to be spurned, proscribed, persecuted, because it comes from north of a given line."[50] In his newspaper, Brownlow pointed out the need of Tennessee for factories for farm machinery, canneries, soap factories, and rolling mills. The state senate, in reply to this message, established a standing committee of five to consider the question of immigration.[51]

In January, 1869, an immigration meeting, planned to form a state society, was held in the capitol. Secretary of State Fletcher, ex-officio member of the state board, presided over the meeting, and described the work of the board. The needs of the state for a diversified system of labor was dwelt upon. A speaker told of the aims of the already extinct German society, and Bokum held out hope by an account of his voluminous correspondence.[52] But the proposed

---

[50] *Whig and Ventilator,* Nov. 18, 1868.
[51] *Acts of Tennessee,* 2nd session, 35th General Assembly, 377.
[52] *Press and Times,* Jan. 13, 1869.

state society was not formed, for the legislature refused to appropriate the necessary subsidy.[53] The work of Bokum and the state board, however, continued,[54] while the presidents of Southern railroads commended Bokum's work, and reduced the fare for immigrants to one cent a mile.[55]

But if the legislature failed to make appropriations for immigration, local interest did not flag. The Knoxville Industrial Association published a pamphlet setting forth the advantages of east Tennessee, and especially Knoxville, to the immigrating laborer or capitalist. Although the association admitted that the soil of east Tennessee would not compare with that of the Western states, it declared that "it quickly responds to kind treatment." But the greater part of the book dealt with the mineral resources and the industrial opportunities of the region. Most of the facts were supplied by Judge O. P. Temple and General J. T. Wilder. The section, said the association, abounded in minerals, and in regard to manufactures, "we offer all the advantages of choice and monopoly of a *New State*." Cotton mills, iron foundries, and marble quarries were needed. The association also set forth the advantage that came from cheap labor in Knoxville; unskilled labor was paid from $0.75 to $1.35 a day, while skilled labor was about the same as in the North. Moreover, the newcomer was assured that he would be welcomed by all classes. East Tennessee, unlike other parts of the state, and of the South, was quiet and peaceable; Ku Klux outrages were all in middle and west Tennessee.[56]

It is evident that east Tennessee was more interested in

---

[53] *Whig and Ventilator,* March 3, 1869.
[54] *Press and Times,* March 22, 1869.
[55] *Ibid.,* Jan. 4 and 22, 1869.
[56] *Facts and Figures concerning the Climate, Manufacturing Advantages and the Agricultural and Mineral Resources of East Tennessee* (Published under the direction of the Knoxville Industrial Association, Knoxville, 1869).

the development of its industrial and mineral resources than in encouraging the immigration of agricultural labor. But the rest of the state desired relief from agricultural disorder. One observer declared that the entire South was inviting immigrants "to help rebuild, on the ruins and ashes of war, the coveted temple of prosperity."[57] With this desire for immigrants, Southern members of Congress supported a bill for subsidizing, by a contract for carrying mail, a steamship company which, supported by Southern immigration societies, would bring European immigrants to the South.[58] In Memphis, planters from west Tennessee assembled to consider the advantages of importing Chinese labor. These, said one Tye Kim Orr, a Chinese who addressed the meeting, could be contracted for in China at from ten to twelve dollars a month and transported to Memphis for less than one hundred and fifty dollars.[59] The planters agreed to raise a million dollars for the project, but even the Radical press opposed the idea of supplanting Christian Negroes by heathen Chinese who "despise your Bible, deride your God, and hate your religion."[60]

By this time the state of Tennessee had passed into the control of the Democrats, but there is no indication that the Conservatives were any less willing than the Radicals to encourage immigration. Among the first acts of the Democratic legislature was the incorporation of the Mississippi Valley Immigration Company, which numbered among its promoters such ex-Confederates as General Gideon J. Pillow and Governor Isham G. Harris. However, it was provided that Chinese would not be imported by the com-

---

[57] Goddard, *Where to Immigrate and Why* (Philadelphia, 1869), 335–36.
[58] *Press and Times*, July 9, 1869.
[59] *Ibid.*, July 15, 1869.
[60] *Ibid.*, September 1, 1869.

pany.[61] This legislature also authorized counties to issue bonds in order to subscribe for stock in the Mediterranean and Oriental Steam Navigation Company which planned to bring immigrants from Europe direct to Southern ports.[62] A further step was taken when the legislature offered to pay this company twenty-five dollars for each immigrant imported to the state.[63] It was evident, however, that the Conservatives were more interested in encouraging the introduction of European immigrants than of Northern capital.

In the second session of the legislature, the act of 1867, creating the board of immigration, was repealed.[64] Seemingly, this was a sign of Conservative disapproval of the Radical program, but in reality, it was only a move to get rid of Radical officeholders. In the next session, the House of Representatives passed a resolution in favor of encouraging immigration,[65] and in December, 1871, the board was reëstablished.[66] It continued its activities until it was merged with the bureau of agriculture, which still keeps up the effort to attract settlers to Tennessee.

---

[61] *Acts of Tennessee,* 1st session, 36th General Assembly, 188.

[62] *Ibid.,* 324–5.

[63] *Ibid.,* 326. Cf., Nashville *Union and American,* May 29, June 2 and 25, 1870.

[64] *Acts of Tennessee,* 2nd session, 36th Assembly, 97.

[65] *Ibid.,* 3rd session, 182.

[66] *Ibid.,* 1st session, 37th General Assembly, 75–77.

THREE

The Propaganda Literature of Confederate Prisons

THE voluminous literature of the American Civil War, ranging in importance from the one hundred and thirty volumes of the *Official Records of the Union and Confederate Armies in the War of the Rebellion* to the latest apocryphal campfire anecdote, illumines every facet of the holocaust for the inquisitive historian. Occupying an interesting place in this literary outpouring are the accounts of those unfortunates who served their country in the prison camps of the enemy. From the summer of 1862 almost to the present day there has come from the press a stream of volumes, articles, and anecdotes about the prisons of the North and the South. The card catalog of the Library of Congress and periodic indexes since 1880 list almost three hundred titles of prison reminiscences.

This prison literature is unique amid the personal memoirs of the Civil War. Most of the ex-soldiers who recounted their wartime experiences did so from motives of personal

Reprinted by permission from the *Journal of Southern History*, 1: 56–66 (February, 1935).

pride or pique, but seldom did they relate their own story to their concepts of the essential nature of the conflict. Generals might write to defend their conduct in a campaign, or soldiers to voice a personal grievance, but the ex-prisoner who took up a reminiscent pen was fighting in a cause. Unlike his fellows the prisoner neither doffed his martial character with his uniform nor permitted time to soften his animosities. Instead he fought on in the determination to convince his readers of the essential brutality of his captors. Prisoners, whether Federal or Confederate, were almost unanimously convinced that their jailors had subjected them to treatment heinously designed to reduce their ranks by starvation and death. Soldiers in the field relegated the horrors of the battlefield to merciful oblivion, but the prisoners remembered their hardships and invented atrocities to fit their hypothesis of "Yankee" or "Rebel" cruelty. More than any other factor, the prisoners' accounts of their sufferings served to keep alive the bitter psychosis of the Civil War.

During and after the war the prisons from Johnson's Island to Andersonville played much the same part that the Belgian atrocities played in the [first] World War. In each case the stories fed the fires of hate and inspired war-crazed peoples with savage impulses. The major difference between them was that the one set of atrocities grew up by accretion while the other was organized and promulgated by official publicity bureaus. Official and expert propagandists in the World War did the work which was usually left to inexpert dabblers in the "Great Rebellion."

Humanitarianism rather than an effort to create atrocity stories, however, led to the first outburst of prison horror stories. In the early part of the Civil War the Federal government adhered to the theory that secession was unconstitutional and its supporters were traitors. Fearing lest it should inadvertently recognize Confederate belligerency, the Lincoln government refused to exchange prisoners. In the Northern papers this attitude was denounced as straining at a technicality. As the government showed no signs of yielding its position, the newspapers of the North had recourse to humanitarian arguments and presented the suffering of the prisoners who were confined in the tobacco warehouses of Richmond after the battle of Bull Run. Northern readers and the government were told that the captives were confined in close rooms "whose poisoned atmosphere is slowly sapping their strength hour by hour"![1] Leaning heavily on their memory of history, the editors borrowed atrocity stories from the War of 1812 and the American Revolution.[2]

By the summer of 1862, when the first accounts by prisoners began to appear, the Northern mind had been conditioned to believe the worst of the South. In the books which saw the light that summer the two arch-fiends of the Confederate prisons were presented to the Northern people. Congressman Alfred Ely, whose curiosity to behold the battle of Manassas had led to his capture and confinement in Richmond, and Colonel Michael Corcoran, self-styled "Hero of Bull Run" and commander of the Irish Sixty-ninth New York militia, each published books which described General W. H. Winder, the commander of prisons in Richmond.[3] The other major figure in prison demonology

---

[1] New York *Times,* Aug. 1, 21, Sept. 30, Oct. 3, 1861; New York *News,* Aug. 2, 19, 20; Alfred Ely, *Journal of Alfred Ely* (New York, 1862), 50, 68, 135; cf. W. B. Hesseltine, *Civil War Prisons* (Columbus, 1930), 9–15, 174.

[2] *Harper's Weekly,* Nov. 2, 1861.

[3] Ely, *Journal of Alfred Ely,* and Michael Corcoran, *The Captivity of General Corcoran, The Only Authentic and Reliable Narrative of the Trials and Sufferings Endured During his Twelve Month's Imprisonment in Richmond and Other Southern Cities* (Philadelphia, 1862).

was Captain Henry Wirz, who was portrayed by W. H. Merrell, a private soldier from New York.⁴ Although Winder was to appear in later accounts as the embodiment of cruelty, neither Ely nor Corcoran recounted any ill treatment at the Confederate's hands. In fact, neither of the prisoners was able to muster a very convincing array of sufferings. Ely recorded that he was well treated by the Confederates; and Corcoran, whose treatment had been much worse, designed his book as a recruiting pamphlet and could not afford to picture his treatment too darkly. Corcoran reserved his censure for the Confederate secretary of war, whom he described as "one of those disgraces to mankind." Merrell, however, had seen a different side of prison life from that revealed to the officers, and he wholeheartedly condemned the Confederates, and especially described Wirz as inhumanly cruel.

There was a definite connection between the prison atrocity stories which appeared during and after the war and the abolitionist propaganda which preceded the conflict. The disciples of Garrison and Weld and Wendell Phillips and Gerritt Smith had labored for a generation to convince the North that slavery produced tyranny, cruelty, and a disregard for human life among the Southerners. Such a belief was readily seized upon by the writers of Northern prison accounts, and people who had wept over *Uncle Tom's Cabin* were soon weeping over the dread story of the Reverend James J. Geer, a Methodist abolitionist who had been imprisoned in Alabama and Georgia. Geer's hatred of the Southern aristocrats was only exceeded by the disgust with which he regarded the "clay-eating" poor whites whom he met. His finer sentiments were reserved

---

⁴ W. H. Merrell, *Five Months in Rebeldom, or Notes from the Diary of a Bull Run Prisoner at Richmond* (Rochester, 1862).

for the oppressed Negroes whose white masters kept them in ignorance. Through Geer's pages the connection between abolition propaganda and the stories of "Rebel" barbarity to prisoners can be clearly traced.[5]

In the summer of 1862, shortly before Geer's diatribe, an exchange was arranged between the two contestants, and the original humane motivation for prison stories disappeared. However, the necessity for proving that the South was peopled by inhuman monsters remained. After a year so many points of difference developed between the agents charged with exchanging prisoners that prisoners again began to be confined in the tobacco warehouses of Richmond or on nearby Belle Isle. Moreover, Secretary Stanton found that soldiers who grew weary of martial discipline took advantage of the exchange cartel and fell into the enemy's hand to obtain paroles. Accordingly, he encouraged the quarrel between the exchange agents and took the first opportunity to end the cartel.[6] The abandonment of exchange was necessary to keep the Northern army up to its full fighting strength.

In order to discourage surrender, the Northern government found it desirable to picture conditions in Southern prisons in the blackest colors. That there would have been little difficulty in finding ample evidence of bad conditions must be apparent when one considers the economic collapse of the Confederacy. As the Southern transportation system broke down Lee's army was frequently without food, and the industrial poverty of the Confederacy rendered it impossible to furnish the soldiers in the field with proper clothing and equipment. Reason could hardly demand that

[5] James J. Geer, *Beyond the Lines; or, a Yankee Loose in Dixie* (Philadelphia, 1863).
[6] For a full discussion of exchange see W. B. Hesseltine, *Civil War Prisons,* 69–113.

a nation accord better treatment to captive enemies than
to the fighting forces. Moreover, as an inevitable circum-
stance, the Confederacy did not assign its best officers or
soldiers to the charge of prison camps. Despite the real efforts which second-rate officers made to obtain supplies for
the prisoners, and the evident intention of the Confederate
government to accord captives the same rations as soldiers
in garrisons, there was much real suffering in Confederate
prisons. Thirteen thousand graves at Andersonville bear
mute evidence to the poverty of the Confederacy, the failure
of its transportation system, and the inefficiency of the
prison system of the South.

Although a portrayal of actual conditions in the South
would have been sufficiently horrible to discourage Northern desertions and surrenders, such a presentation would
have been but additional arguments to Northern people
that exchanges should be resumed. Faced with this situation the war department inaugurated a new phase of prison
literature. Official propaganda was undertaken to convince
the North that exchange was impossible—that it had been
stopped by the South—and that the Southerners were actu-
ated by a determination to destroy the lives of the prisoners in their hands. Well-edited copies of the bickering
correspondence between the exchange agents were issued
to the press; and the agents themselves wrote letters to the
papers explaining why exchange had stopped.[7] Along with
this went official reports on conditions in the Confederate
prisons. The first of them was a report to the surgeon-
general on a boat load of sick prisoners for whom a special
exchange had been arranged. These prisoners were de-

---

[7] New York *Times,* Nov. 10, 1863; *National Intelligencer,* Dec. 2,
3, 7, 1863; cf. *Official Records of the Union and Confederate Armies
in the War of the Rebellion* (Washington, 1880 ff.), Ser. 2, VI, 590
and *passim.*

scribed as filthy, covered with vermin, and starved.[8] This report was given wide circulation.[9]

In the spring of the following year, Secretary Stanton urged the Committee on the Conduct of the War to visit a hospital for returned prisoners at Annapolis and make a report which would show to the Northern people and the "civilized world," the "enormity of the crimes committed by the rebels toward our prisoners." The secretary was sure that the committee would find "a deliberate system of savage and barbarous treatment."[10]

Thus inspired and instructed, the Committee, which was the chief agency in all Northern propaganda, visited Annapolis and prepared an official report on all southern prisons. In thirty pages and eight photographs it summarized the testimony of the prisoners and offered ample proof of Stanton's contention. The horrors of Libby Prison and the infamous Belle Isle in Richmond were set forth in full detail. The eight pictures were masterpieces of photography and of the artist's imagination. Although two were of men who had died before the committee visited the hospital, and another was of a soldier who had not been in prison,[11] the committee wasted no space on such irrelevant details.[12] Immediately the report was published and given the widest possible circulation.[13]

Official endorsement of prison propaganda made the recounting of atrocity stories an act of high patriotism. Not to be outdone by the Committee on the Conduct of the

---

[8] *Official Records*, Ser. 2, VI, 474-476.
[9] *National Intelligencer*, Nov. 20, 1863.
[10] *Official Records*, Ser. 2, VII, 110-111.
[11] See Jefferson Davis to James Lyons, in *Southern Historical Society Papers*, I (1876).
[12] House of Representatives, 38 Cong., 1 Sess., Rept. No. 67.
[13] Cf. Frank Moore (ed.), *The Rebellion Record* (New York, 1864–68), VIII, 80–98.

War, the United States Sanitary Commission added propaganda to its other and more humane activities. Almost immediately after the official report the Commission appointed
a committee headed by a Dr. Ellerslie Wallace, of New
York, to make a study of the prisons in both North and
South. Secretary Stanton regarded this development with
a suspicious fear that the Sanitary Commission's investigators might not confirm the horrors found by the official
propagandists.[14] However, the committee proceeded with
its work, visited several Northern hospitals, and interviewed
returned prisoners. By early fall, they had a report ready
which surpassed in literary excellence and in vividness of
account the best efforts of the Committee on the Conduct
of the War.

The Sanitary Commission's *Narrative of Privations and
Sufferings of United States Officers and Soldiers While Prisoners of War in the Hands of the Rebel Authorities*[15] was
soon reprinted and given wide circulation by the Loyal
League, another patriotic propaganda organization. With a
gullibility possible only in war conditions, the committee
listed every atrocity story which had been concocted to that
time. Like the House committee's report, this one contained
eight pictures of alleged prisoners whose naked bodies
showed the ravages of prison-contracted disease. Beginning
with a description of the robbery practiced by the Confederates at the time of capture, the *Narrative* carried the prisoners along the gory march from the battlefield to Richmond's tobacco warehouses. In the committee's mind there
was no doubt that the Confederates deliberately deprived
the prisoners of furniture, clothing, warmth and food. The
rulers of the prisons, especially General Winder, were ex-

---

[14] *Official Records*, Ser. 2, VII, 188–189.
[15] Philadelphia, 1864. It was reviewed in the *National Intelligencer*, Oct. 7, 1864. Cf. *Harper's Weekly*, Oct. 29, 1864.

coriated as worse than beasts, and the committee concluded, after exhibiting their museum of horrors, that "a predetermined plan, originating somewhere in the rebel counsels," was responsible for the brutality. In contrast, the committee pictured the pleasant lives and even luxurious surroundings which characterized the prisons of the North.

The effect of these two books was seen in the absence of any further writing on the subject of prisons until after the end of the war. From the time of these publications until within a few months of Appomattox the potential *raconteurs* of prison experiences were in Andersonville and other Southern prisons and there was no opportunity for them to produce accounts of their adventures. However, with the close of the war there began a rush of publication which continued until the World War.

Stimulating the prisoners to recount their experiences was the trial and execution of Henry Wirz in August, 1865. When Andersonville was established in 1864, Wirz, who had lost an arm in the Confederate service, was assigned to the command of the interior of the prison. Captured at the close of the war, he was confined in the Old Capitol prison in Washington, where he was tried by a military court on charges of excessive cruelty, of the murder of prisoners in his charge, and of conspiring with the leaders of the Confederacy to reduce by death the prison population of the South. The presiding officer of the military court was General Lew Wallace, soon to write a novel on the life of Christ. But a contemplation of the career of the world's greatest Martyr did not even inspire the general to Pilate's renunciatory gesture. His aid was freely given to the prosecution which was conducted by Colonel N. P. Chipman of the Judge Advocate General's office. No man in the North was more thoroughly victimized by war psychosis than was Chipman, and he conducted the prosecution with a zeal which ignored the rules of evidence and did not hesitate to suborn perjury. Witnesses whose characters could not bear close examination gave testimony according to their instructions. In lurid language they described the terrors of life under a Georgia summer's sun. Wirz and Winder were condemned as fiends, and eyewitness accounts of murders were given. Disease and death had stalked the prison camp while food, clothing and shelter were entirely lacking. Wirz was found guilty of wanton murder and of conspiring with Jefferson Davis and Robert E. Lee to destroy the lives of his charges. November 10, 1865, the unfortunate victim of war's hatreds was hanged in the yard of the Old Capitol prison, on the site now occupied by the Supreme Court building.

Without the Wirz trial the literature of Confederate prisons would have had a less interesting future. The voluminous report of the trial was published by the government[16] and immediately became a source book for writers of "memoirs." During the next two years twenty-eight books and articles came from the press setting forth the horrors of life in southern prison camps. A number of these were written by witnesses at the Wirz trial, and all of them bore unmistakable evidence that the authors had borrowed heavily from the official report. Within the next five years twenty more books were published. All of them were digests of the Wirz trial evidence.[17]

This outburst of prison literature was not due solely to the desire of the ex-prisoners to set down their real or imagined experiences. These years were full of bitter

---

[16] *The Trial of Henry Wirz*, 40 Cong., 2 Sess., House Ex. Doc. No. 23.

[17] These figures, and those that follow, are based upon the copyright records and the *Periodical Index*. Many other books, articles, and newspaper accounts were published. It is assumed that the copyrighted and indexed publications reflect the general interest in the subject of prisons.

struggle over the treatment of the South in Reconstruction. The writers were all convinced that a record of their sufferings might contribute to the punishment of the South. "The magnanimity of our people is beyond question, and our enemies acknowledge it," declared one writer. "We must neither be too lenient or too severe. To the *leaders* who precipitated us into four years of bloodshed and war, the severest punishment which the law can give; but to the poor misguided masses, that clemency which only noble people are capable of exercising."[18] Another writer, opposing Andrew Johnson's wholesale pardons, declared his enmity to the "Slave Oligarchy" which was being restored to citizenship. "I send out this book," he avowed, "trusting that whatever influence it may exercise will aid in bringing the guilty leaders of Treason to just punishment for their enormous crimes against humanity."[19] The interest in such accounts and the use made of them in the bitter fights of Reconstruction is evidenced in the political oratory of the day. Republican speakers rang the welkin with stories of prison atrocities. No group in America furnished more gore for the bloody shirt than ex-prisoners of war.

In 1869 the Republican House of Representatives, perceiving the value of the prisons in politics, appointed a committee to make an investigation of the subject. After taking testimony from some three thousand witnesses, the committee published a report which immediately became a new textbook for both political speakers and polemical writers. The committee was frank in avowing its purpose to condemn the whole system of slavery and the resultant barbarism of the South. "Rebel cruelty demands an enduring

---

[18] A. O. Abbott, *Prison Life in the South* (New York, 1865), 206.
[19] A. C. Roach, *The Prisoner of War and How Treated* (Indianapolis, 1865), 3–4.

truthful record, stamped with the National authority,"
declared the investigators. As in every other case, the committee was convinced of a diabolical Confederate plot to kill
prisoners.[20]

Although the interest in prisons continued among politicians for a number of years, and even as late as 1876 James
G. Blaine could use it in his futile effort to climb to the
White House, the number of books written by prisoners
declined. However, early in the eighties a new reason was
found for publishing accounts of prison experiences. As the
veterans of the Civil War began their series of pension raids
on the national treasury, the number of prison reminiscences suddenly increased. Prisoners found themselves at a
disadvantage in proving they had suffered injury during the
war. There were no surgeons in the prisons to certify to
disability contracted therein, and prisoners found difficulty
in getting two competent witnesses for their alleged injuries.
As if to overwhelm the nation's legislators with a flood of
sympathy the ex-prisoners thumbed their copies of the Wirz
trial and the congressional report and set their pens to re-
cording the events of their horrible sufferings.[21] In the
decade after 1878 thirty-one books and articles appeared to
plead for pensions, and in the following five years thirty-
nine more such items appeared in the publishers' lists. From
1892 to 1901 another thirty-two saw the light of day, followed by fifty-one more before 1910. The subject was kept
constantly alive, and the number of private pension bills for
prisoners, and the eventual modification of the pension
laws, were the tangible results.

---

[20] *Treatment of Prisoners of War by the Rebel Authorities,* House
of Representatives, 40 Cong., 3 Sess., Rept. No. 85.

[21] John L. Ransom, *Andersonville Diary* (Auburn, 1881), 163; A.
Cooper, *In and Out of Rebel Prisons* (Oswego, 1888), 346–347; S. S.
Boggs, *Eighteen Months a Prisoner under the Rebel Flag* (Loving-
ton, Ill., 1889), 63.

Most of this writing was, of course, purely ephemeral, but some of the books had a wide circulation. Among the more important, both from the standpoint of its bitterness and its influence, was the *Soldier's Story of His Captivity at Andersonville, Belle Isle, and Other Rebel Prisons,* by Warren Lee Goss,[22] which was used with great effect by the congressional committee in its report in 1869. Another widely circulated work was the product of the facile pen of a Toledo *Blade* journalist, John McElroy. His *Andersonville, A Story of Rebel Military Prisons*[23] was perhaps the best written of the entire list, although it contained more than the usual share of inaccuracies. McElroy attacked Wirz with venom and presented a story of "Rebel" cruelty which must have been convincing to his credulous readers. This work had perhaps the largest circulation of any prison account. A. O. Abbott's *Prison Life in the South* related the experiences of an officer in Libby and Macon, Georgia, and John L. Ransom's *Andersonville Diary* was widely read and frequently quoted.

In the list of prison literature there are a few freakish works. One pamphlet was written as a begging device and sold from door to door by its crippled author. There was no internal evidence that the writer ever saw a Southern prison, and he had neglected to copy either of the official source books.[24] Another writer, who made a business of lecturing about his experiences, published a book which recounted his stay in various prisons. Reversing the order in which the prisons in the South were established, he arrived at Andersonville, according to his story, a full year before the

---

[22] Boston, 1869.
[23] Toledo, 1879.
[24] *A History of George W. Murray and his Long Confinement at Andersonville, Georgia* (Hartford).

Georgia prison was established.[25] But perhaps the most interesting writer was the ingenious if not prolific John W. Urban, who published the same book under three different titles, the only other differences being in the pictures and the binding.[26] Such charlatanry was different only in degree from that practiced by a host of imaginary writers who, for pensions, for political ends, or for war purposes, copied official propaganda to incite and keep alive a hatred of the South.[27]

---

[25] Ralph Q. Bates, *Billy and Dick from Andersonville Prison to the White House* (Santa Cruz, Calif., 1910).

[26] Urban, *My Experiences Mid Shot and Shell and in Rebel Den,* and *In Defense of the Union, or, Through Shot and Shell and Prison Pen,* and *Battlefield and Prison and Prison Pen* (all, Lancaster, Pa., 1882). Only slightly different is his *Through the War and Thrice a Prisoner in Rebel Dungeons* (Philadelphia, 1892).

[27] For a bibliography of prison literature, cf. W. B. Hesseltine, *Civil War Prisons,* 259–282; see also 242, 247–257.

FOUR

Economic Factors in the Abandonment of Reconstruction

BY common consent, President Rutherford B. Hayes's withdrawal of Federal troops from the South has been accepted as the end of Reconstruction. The President's action, however, was but the outward and visible symbol of an already accomplished revolution in Northern sentiment. For a number of years the Northern voters had been coming to realize that the effort to force the South into the Northern political mold was both costly and futile.

Commentators on the politics of the Reconstruction period have ascribed this reversal of opinion to the rise of new interests among the Northern electorate, or have dismissed it with a remark that the people had grown tired of the Southern question in politics. Such an interpretation fails to consider that Reconstruction itself was an economic as well as a political problem, and that it was not until the political program failed to bring economic results that the control of the South was returned to the Southern white man.

Reprinted by permission from the *Mississippi Valley Historical Review*, 22: 191–210 (September, 1935).

Fundamentally, Reconstruction was the method by which the "Masters of Capital" sought to secure their victory over the vanquished "Lords of the Manor," and through which they expected to exploit the resources of the Southern states. Long before the war was over cotton speculators, acting as the vanguard of an economic army, followed the advancing Federal armies and annoyed commanders from the Red River to the Potomac by their persistent efforts to carry on trade with the South. Behind the lines, less mobile entrepreneurs calculated the possibility of carrying the Northern economic system into the South at the close of hostilities. In the first months after Appomattox, businessmen in the North looked for immediate profits from the return of peace and endorsed General Ulysses S. Grant's leniency and President Andrew Johnson's plans for a speedy restoration of the Southern state. One of Grant's aides-de-camp found that in the summer of 1865 "all the sober, substantial men" of New York, St. Louis, and Washington were in favor of Johnson's policy.[1] Impressed with the necessity for Southern industrial rehabilitation, the New York *Commercial and Financial Chronicle* ingratiatingly assured the South that the Northern people contemplated no oppression but would accord the Southern states an early readmission to the Union.[2]

Totally ignoring the psychoses of the conquered Southerners, Northern financial circles seemed to believe that the South would "treat political questions as secondary" until industrial recuperation had been accomplished. This recovery, of course, would be the result of Northern capital, in the hands of Northern men, flowing into the South.

---

[1] Adam Badeau to E. B. Washburne, October 20, 1865, E. B. Washburne MSS. (in Library of Congress).

[2] New York *Commercial and Financial Chronicle,* July 1, 1865.

"There can be no way so sure to make the late rebels of the South loyal men and good citizens," declared the New York organ of the financiers, "as to turn their energies to the pursuits of peace, and the accumulation of wealth." When goods from Southern factories appeared in the New York markets, they caused this journal to remember that in 1860 there had been 350 woolen mills and 180 cotton mills in the South and that the total value of Southern manufactured goods had been over $238,000,000! "Now," proclaimed the hopeful editor, "Northern men, accustomed to business, have gone South and will give a new impetus" to industrial development.[3]

In order to encourage Northern men to migrate to the South, commercial newspapers began to advertise the South as the nation's new land of opportunity. The abundance of land, the manufacturing possibilities, the climate, soil, water-power, and timber of the South came in for extensive exposition, and the figures of the South's exports in 1860— over two hundred million dollars—was dangled before the eyes of the Northern people. The South was assured that an immigration of new and energetic people would begin as soon as the Johnsonian governments were fully established.[4]

Such roseate dreams of a golden harvest in the South were rudely shattered when the Southerners began to take stock of their own position. In the first days after the war planters welcomed ex-officers of the Union armies who came to purchase cotton plantations,[5] but few of these adventurers were successful either in handling Negroes or in living harmoniously with their white neighbors.[6] Political differences which

---

[3] *Ibid.*, August 26, 1865.
[4] *Ibid.*, September 2, October 14, 1865.
[5] W. L. Fleming, *Civil War and Reconstruction in Alabama* (New York, 1905), 322–23.
[6] Allan Nevins, *Emergence of Modern America* (New York, 1927), 22–23.

engendered social ostracism and even physical violence soon developed, and the Northerners returned to their homes none the richer for their experience. Instead of welcoming immigrants and making provisions to receive migrating capitalists, the provisional governments under Johnson's program showed more interest in attempting to solve the economic problems of an agrarian area.

Some efforts, however, were made by several of the states to attract immigrants, and boards of immigration were set up by the Reconstruction governments.[7] But only in Tennessee was there a real enthusiasm for the task. There the east Tennesseans, who had never been a part of the cotton kingdom but had long nursed secret ambitions to become industrialized, controlled the state and made a serious effort to entice Northern capital. Newspapers appealed to Tennesseans to advertise their lands, mill and factory sites, and mines in order to attract merchants, manufacturers, and bankers—"the very class of men . . . whose help is needed in developing the wealth of our great State."[8] The legislature generously chartered a number of "immigration" companies in order to assist expected immigrants, and in December 1867 a state board of immigration was established. The board employed an energetic commissioner to advertise the state's resources in the North and in Europe.[9] In Radical Missouri there was also a welcome to immigrants, but in other parts of the South a suspicion of the political motives

---

[7] Hermann Bokum, *The Tennessee Handbook and Immigrants Guide* . . . (Philadelphia, 1868), 129; B. J. Loewenberg, "Efforts to Encourage Immigration into the South, 1865–1900," in *South Atlantic Quarterly* (Durham, 1902–), XXXIII (1934), 363–85.

[8] Nashville *Daily Press and Times,* January 1, 1867.

[9] *Acts of Tennessee,* 34 General Assembly, 1 Sess., 74; *ibid.,* 2 Sess., 119–21, 311, 411; 35 Gen. Assemb., 1 Sess., 11–12, 24, 30, 303, 317. For a fuller account see W. B. Hesseltine, "Tennessee's Invitation to Carpetbaggers."

of the migrants caused them to be either ostracized or mistreated.[10]

The attitude of the Southerners was not long in being reported to Congress. "Loyal" citizens, Unionists, and Northern immigrants appealed to congressmen for protection against the "frightful spirit of lawlessless extant among the late rebels." From Virginia to Texas plaintive letters to congressmen told the story of bad treatment.[11] Already the Radicals in Congress had determined to force Negro suffrage on the South in order to maintain the Republican party in power. Under the added stimulus of the anguished cries of businessmen both North and South the congressional program of Reconstruction was formulated. (The Fourteenth Amendment would protect the property of Union men in the South[12] and by disfranchising the leaders of the old agricultural South would enable "loyal" men and Negroes to enact the legislation which would protect the Northern capitalist in exploiting the South.) When the Southern states rejected the amendment, Congress proceeded to carry its program into effect. Only Radical Tennessee, whose arms were outstretched in welcome to invading capital, was admitted to representation in Congress.

The passage of the Reconstruction Act of March 2, 1867, renewed the hope of a migration of capital and labor to the South.[13] Union men in Virginia looked forward to the migration of "Northern men with capital and enterprise to

---

[10] Nashville *Daily Press and Times,* February 13, 21, 28, March 19, April 29, 1867.

[11] B. Wardwell to B. F. Butler, February 26, 1866; William Alexander to George Gibbs, June 28, 1866, B. F. Butler MSS. (in Library of Congress).

[12] Roscoe Conkling in County of San Mateo *v.* Southern Pacific Railway Company, 13. *Fed.* 722 ff.

[13] E. A. Comstock MS. Diary, March 28, 1867 (in Library of Congress).

develop the resources of our fields and forests." Moreover a political purpose would be served, for such people, wrote a citizen of Richmond, "by their social intercourse and votes . . . would do much to neutralize the prejudices and influence of parties inimical to the Government."[14] When General James A. Longstreet renounced his Confederate heresies in favor of Southern prosperity, Massachusett's Ben Butler hastened to welcome him to the Radical fold. If all Southerners would take Longstreet's views, Butler foresaw that "harmony of feeling, community of interest, unity of action as well as homogeneity of institutions" would follow to produce national well being.[15]

But Longstreet was almost alone in his decision to "accept the results of the war" and the military governments in the South could do little to further the North's exploitation of its southern colony. Men who had gone south for economic reasons took advantage of the changed situation to recoup their losses in politics, and others came from the North solely for the plums of office. But the Union men and Northerners in the South continued to find themselves at a disadvantage. The property of loyalists was not safe in the courts, and Ben Butler soon heard appeals from the Unionists to turn the courts over to loyal men. "The Northern man will not come here unless his capital is safe," declared one of Butler's Georgia informants.[16] From Texas it was reported that rebel leaders were growing rich but that there was no hope for Union men.[17] On the advice of the "best financiers" Butler decided to abandon his own extensive investments[18] in the South, although he contemplated, according to one news-

---

[14] S. C. Hayes to Butler, March 28, 30, 1867, Butler MSS.
[15] Butler to James Longstreet, June 19, 1867, *ibid.*
[16] Caleb Thompson to Butler, July 16, 1867, *ibid.*
[17] Anthony M. Dignowity to Butler, November 30, 1867, *ibid.*
[18] T. Pearson to Butler, and endorsement, October 9, 1867, *ibid.*

paper, a bill which would prevent disfranchised rebels from holding office on railroads or chartered companies.[19]

The New York *Commercial and Financial Chronicle,* a consistent supporter of Johnson's policy, soon found that congressional Reconstruction was paralyzing business and unnecessarily prolonging Southern industrial prostration. If Negro majorities controlled the state legislatures, the paper warned, capital would stay out of the section.[20] Despite this analysis, the Radicals pursued their course and blamed bad conditions on President Johnson. When the Tennessee legislature met in December 1867, Governor William G. Brownlow, the "Fighting Parson," reported that "men of capital and enterprise" had not come into the state in the expected numbers. This was due to Andrew Johnson's "insane policy" of holding out to "pestilential disloyalists" the hope that they would be restored to power.[21] Butler agreed with this contention and declared that only a new president could insure the property rights of Northerners in the South.[22]

During the campaign of 1868 Democratic orators took pains to assert that peace and prosperity could come only through the abandonment of congressional Reconstruction,[23] but Republicans, saying little of the economic rehabilitation of the South, made much of the Southerner's vindictiveness towards the Union men and loyal Negroes of the South. Ku Klux outrages and Democratic murders constituted the main theme of the Republicans, despite the fact that these very stories would serve as a deterrent to capital seeking Southern investments. In their belief, inter-

---

[19] Clipping from [Boston?] *Traveler,* December 14, 1867, *ibid.*
[20] New York *Commercial and Financial Chronicle,* January 18, 1868.
[21] *Acts of Tennessee,* 35 Gen. Assemb., 1 Sess., appendix, 15–16.
[22] Endorsement on Thompson letter, see *ante,* n. 16.
[23] New York *Times,* September 14, 1868.

est in manufactures and agriculture would "supersede the
excitement of the caucus" and the South would "turn all
her energies to . . . developing her immense resources" as
soon as the election was over. When friction ceased, business
would "spring to its feet . . . manufacture . . . unchain her
idle wheels," and "the cotton and rice plantations of the
South . . . vie with the cornfields of the West."[24] In the end,
the businessman of the North voted for the Republicans,
not because he was convinced by this reasoning but because
the party stood for the payment of the national debt in
gold.[25]

Republican success in the election of 1868 was widely
interpreted as settling the disorders in the South. "The
election of Grant and Colfax means peace," cried Tennessee's Brownlow. "It means that carpetbaggers are not to be
molested in Tennessee, that capital, coming to us from
abroad, whether of brains or hands, or money, is not to be
spurned, proscribed, persecuted, because it comes from
north of a given line."[26] According to Horace Greeley, immigrants could now be safely invited into the country, and
two-thirds of them would "go to build up the waste places
of the South."[27] Greeley also noticed that the election would
insure the reconstruction of Virginia where Northern capital was waiting for a favorable government before it advanced money for the completion of a railroad from the
Ohio to the Chesapeake Bay.[28] Even from ex-Confederates
in the South there came echoes of the same conclusion. One
Alabamian, who had served in the Confederate army and
had voted against Grant, wrote to Butler that his state

---

[24] New York *Tribune*, October 20, 1868.
[25] Charles H. Coleman, *The Election of 1868* (New York, 1933),
24 ff., 372–74.
[26] Knoxville *Whig and Rebel Ventilator*, November 18, 1868.
[27] New York *Tribune*, November 10, 1868.
[28] *Ibid.*, November 6, 1868.

wanted to "induce men of capital and skill" to come in. "If you are desirous for the welfare of the South, and wish to be personally highly remunerated and at the same time become a public benefactor, you can accomplish these objects better than in any other manner by inducing your men of means and skill to invest their money and skill" in the South.[29] John Letcher, erstwhile war-governor of Virginia, looked forward to a speedy settlement of the political controversies in order that the prosperity of his section might be assured.[30]

President Grant entered office determined to end the conflict in the South. His first action on Reconstruction was to submit the constitutions of Virginia, Texas, and Mississippi to a vote without the obnoxious clauses which disfranchised the Confederate leaders. This action was immediately hailed with satisfaction, and Northern businessmen looked to the completion of political reconstruction as the beginning of Southern prosperity. In Virginia, the Conservatives of the state rapidly formed a party pledged to the acceptance of the Fifteenth Amendment, to the development of industry, and to the encouragement of immigration. "In short," commented Greeley, "Virginia, having had enough of Civil War and devastation, is about to subordinate political strife to industrial progress and material prosperity, and thus advance to a future of power and wealth undreamed of in her past."[31] On the eve of the Virginia election, General J. D. Imboden, who had served his state from Bull Run to Appomattox, wrote to the *Tribune* that Northern men were safe and welcome in Virginia. Millions of white men were needed to develop the state's resources.[32] There was no

---

[29] Thomas Peters to Butler, November 14, 1868, Butler MSS.

[30] John Letcher to E. B. Washburne, November 19, 1868, Elihu B. Washburne MSS.

[31] New York *Tribune,* May 8, 1869.

[32] *Ibid.,* May 22, 1869.

doubt that Virginia was succumbing to the lure of profits. In May, 1869, General Lee visited Washington on railroad business and called at the White House to assure Grant that Virginia favored the Fifteenth Amendment and Negro suffrage![33]

The Virginia elections were the quietest that had taken place in the South since secession, but the resultant Conservative victory struck terror into the ranks of the Radical Republican politicians. On economic issues the newly elected governor, Gilbert C. Walker, was in thorough accord with the masters of capital who were backing the Republican party in the North. His party accepted Negro suffrage and stood for the industrialization of the state, yet there was little doubt that the Virginia Conservatives would unite with the Northern Democracy in national elections. Faced with this certainty, Republican politicians sought for an excuse to keep the state under military government, while Walker hurried to Washington to lay his case before Grant and to promise that the Conservatives would not recant their promises to ratify the Fifteenth Amendment.[34]

The dissatisfaction of the politicians with this development was soon revealed. Although the politicians represented the masters of capital who were interested in tariffs, railroads, and the exploitation of the South, they were themselves more interested in the preservation of their party in power. The only member of Grant's cabinet who was a politician was Secretary of the Treasury George S. Boutwell, who immediately declared his unalterable opposition to

---

[33] *Ibid.*, May 3, 1869; Adam Badeau, *Grant in Peace* (Hartford, 1887), 26–27; Robert E. Lee, Jr., *Recollections and Letters of General Robert E. Lee* (New York, 1904), 349.

[34] New York *Tribune*, July 12, 1869; cf. James F. Rhodes, *History of the United States from the Compromise of 1850* (New York, 1910–19), VI, 303–304.

the Virginia results.[35] Publicly, he counseled caution, taking, according to the disgusted Greeley, "more account of the unity and coherence of the Republican party than of the triumph of its cardinal principle."[36] Intent upon preventing a repetition of this miscarriage, Boutwell condemned the Conservative party in Mississippi and persuaded Grant to repudiate his brother-in-law, Louis Dent, whom the Conservatives had nominated for governor. So great was the pressure of the politicians that Grant yielded to their wishes in Texas and threw the weight of the administration's influence into the scales against the Conservative candidate.[37]

Boutwell's attitude foreshadowed the imminent separation between those who would exploit the South for political advantage and those who sought a field for economic expansion. Moderate Republicans, such as James A. Garfield, deplored the violence that existed in Texas and Mississippi at the same time they commended the peaceful reconstruction of Virginia.[38] Radicals of the Butler stripe, on the other hand, were convinced that Virginia had deceived the Republican party. The victory of the Conservatives in Tennessee in 1869 and the action of the Georgia legislature in expelling its Negro members seemed to them sufficient indication that the South was not yet reconciled to the Union. Butler's own losses in three Southern investments had convinced him that capital was not yet safe in the South.[39]

---

[35] James A. Garfield to J. D. Cox, July 19, 1869, J. A. Garfield MSS. (in Library of Congress).

[36] New York *Tribune,* July 14, 15, 16, 1869.

[37] S. S. Cox, *Three Decades of Federal Legislation* (Providence, 1885), 529–30, 576; see also New York *Tribune,* August 12, 1869.

[38] Garfield to J. S. Black, July 24, 1869, Garfield MSS.

[39] Butler to F. J. Butler, January 18, 1869, Butler MSS.

After the election of 1868 Horace Greeley had become the principal exponent of Northern infiltration into the South. In much the same manner that he had formerly urged the male youth to seek the West, he now devoted the columns of the powerful New York *Tribune* to urging groups to settle in the South. Southern land which had been worth twenty dollars an acre before the war and would soon be worth that again could be bought for one or two dollars an acre. Advising settlement in colonies, Greeley estimated that three thousand colonists in Florida, five thousand each in Alabama, Louisiana, Arkansas, and Mississippi, and ten thousand each in Virginia, North Carolina, and Texas would make the South Republican and deliver it from "the nightmare which now oppresses . . . politics and industry."[40] Within the South, said Greeley, there was a division between two classes on the issues of reconstruction. The "landholders, merchants and men of property, with all who are inclined to industry and thrift," were opposed by a "decreasing faction of sore-heads and malignants." In issue after issue of his paper, the expansionist editor carried articles by the first class of Southerners setting forth the advantages of various sections of the South for immigrants and for capital investments.[41] As the Virginia question arose, Greeley reiterated that the South was begging for immigrants and for Northern capital, and a *Tribune* correspondent wandered through the South gathering details of the wealth awaiting Northern enterprise. North Carolina offered cheap land, docile laborers, ample timber resources, and political peace. In South Carolina there were woolen mills and cotton factories. Tennessee had blast furnaces already established by Northern capital, and there were rich opportunities for in-

---

40 New York *Tribune*, December 16, 1868.
41 *Ibid.*, January 19, 28, February 1, 1869, *et passim.*

vestment in mines of iron, coal, zinc, and copper. The South, editorialized the *Tribune,* had shown a general willingness to come back into the Union on the Greeley platform of "universal amnesty and universal suffrage."[42]

The fundamental issues between the politicians and the businessmen were clearly brought out in an open letter from Greeley to Butler. Appealing to Butler's practical sense, the editor showed that the Radical program of proscription and disfranchisement had retarded business. In reply, Butler declared that Greeley's course had encouraged the rebels so that they had gained the upper hand in Tennessee and Georgia. In these states, the people had deceived the Republican party. Conditions would have been better if a half dozen leading rebels had been hanged at the end of the war.[43]

In the winter of 1869–1870 these divergent views were advanced in the debates over the admission of Virginia and over the treatment to be accorded to recalcitrant Georgia. In the end, Virginia was admitted, although the Radicals had many misgivings. Georgia was remanded to military rule. Not even Greeley could defend the action of the "rebel element" in Georgia and both Moderates and Radicals were agreed that outrages against Republicans in the South should stop. As a means of stopping them, both elements heralded the ratification of the Fifteenth Amendment and supported the "Force Bill" of 1870 which would guarantee the right of suffrage to the Negroes. To the Radicals the martial law in Georgia and the Enforcement Act were means of getting Republican majorities in the South; to the Moderates, the hope of eventual peace carried with it the

---

[42] *Ibid.,* May 15, June 14, 24, 25, July 5, 14, 24, August 13, September 21, October 30, 1869.
[43] *Ibid.,* November 27, December 16, 20, 1869.

promise of a prosperous infiltration of Northern business in the South. In Greeley's opinion, it was time to "have done with Reconstruction." "The country is . . . sick of it," he added. "So long as any State is held in abeyance, it will be plausibly urged that the Republicans are afraid to trust the People. Let us give every State to herself, and then punish any who violate or defy the guaranties of public and personal rights now firmly imbedded in the Constitution."[44]

Although Moderates and Radicals had agreed on the Fifteenth Amendment and the Enforcement Act there were differences between them on the method to be pursued in the future. Radical politicians of the school of Conkling, Morton, Chandler, and Butler looked to the power of the President to enforce the law, while Greeley and the Moderates continued to appeal to the South's hopes of prosperity as a means of producing peace. The advantages of immigration, the possibility of industrial development, and the potentialities of the South's mineral wealth were constantly kept before the Southerners.[45]

Despite Greeley's appeals, the majority of the Southern states offered few inducements to Northern migrants. The competition of Western lands prevented new agricultural groups entering the South,[46] while cases of violence were constantly reported which discouraged those who might have thought of carrying their capital into Southern industry. Greeley's Washington correspondent suspected that most of the outrage stories were "manufactured and published in the North to further the personal designs of unscrupulous and ambitious men."[47] Yet a *Tribune* agent in the South in the summer of 1870 found the Ku Klux in

44 *Ibid.,* April 18, 1870.
45 *Ibid.,* April 30, May 23, June 4, 17, 1870.
46 New York *Times,* May 31, 1870.
47 New York *Tribune,* June 22, 1870.

undeniable operation.[48] Throughout the congressional campaigns the North was flooded with atrocity stories, and a congressional investigation in the succeeding winter gave ample evidence that the Klan was terrorizing the South.[49] The results of these outrages was the passage of two more acts which would keep the South orderly: the Federal Elections Act of February 28, and the Ku Klux Act of April 20, 1871.

In contemplating the Southern scene, Moderates found themselves forced to admit that violence and political murders prevented business recovery and impelled the government to take action. Greeley, however, continued to advise moderation and amnesty as a more suitable means of inducing the Southerners to accept a real economic reconstruction.[50] In Congress, Garfield doubted the constitutionality of the "Force Acts" and declared that the legislation was "working on the very edge of the Constitution." Nevertheless, he found that a "kind of party terrorism" forced all Republicans to vote for the measures.[51] To J. D. Cox, Grant's former secretary of the interior, it seemed that Congress was pursuing the wrong course in attempting to conquer the South. "Capital and intelligence must lead," he told Garfield. "Only Butler and W. Philips would make a wilderness and call it peace." The party should organize and appeal to the "thinking and influential native Southerners" —the "intelligent, well-to-do, and controlling class" of Southern whites.[52]

Soon after the passage of the Ku Klux Act, Greeley sent

---

[48] *Ibid.,* August 3, September 30, October 25, 1870.
[49] *Senate Executive Documents,* 41 Cong., 3 Sess., no. 16, pt. 2.
[50] New York *Tribune,* December 9, 16, 1870, March 15, 1871.
[51] Garfield to J. D. Cox, March 23, April 8; Garfield to A. B. Hinsdale, March 30, 1871, Garfield MSS.
[52] J. D. Cox to Garfield, March 27, April 1, 1871, *ibid.*

correspondents into the South to study conditions. The reporters found that the Klan was overrunning South Carolina, but that the carpetbaggers, who were levying taxes upon industry and wealth, were giving partial justification for the outrages.[53] Late in May, Greeley himself traveled through the Southwest to speak on the glories of industry at the Texas State Fair. The New Yorker's speeches inspired the editor of the New Orleans *Price Current* to comment that the industrial doctrines of Greeley and Seward had conquered the South. "It is the true duty of the South," declared the New Orleans editor, "to cultivate all those industries the want of which has enslaved her."[54] But Greeley had concluded from his observations that the South would not be prosperous until the carpetbaggers with their taxes and the Ku Klux with its violence had both been driven out. The South, said Greeley, was suffering from "decayed aristocracy and imported rascality."[55]

From the time of his Southern trip Greeley was a candidate for the presidency. From what he had seen in the South, however, he changed his earlier ideas that capital would enter the South. The high taxes which the carpetbag and Negro governments had imposed were sufficient to prevent the migration of capital, but the editor believed that prosperity might yet come through the efforts of the Southerners themselves. There were millions of acres in the South which might be sold to immigrants, and the proceeds devoted to the development of local resources. The primary needs of the South, as Greeley came to see it, were more people, more skill, more energy, and greater thrift. The South did not need more capital than would naturally flow

[53] New York *Tribune*, April 26, 28, May 2, 17, 1871.
[54] *Ibid.*, June 2, 12, 1871.
[55] *Ibid.*, July 19, 1871, February 20, 1872.

into it if the people should use their available resources. To his earlier program of universal amnesty and universal suffrage, the editor added the proposal that the South should work out its own salvation by encouraging Northern immigration, driving out carpetbaggers, and freeing the land from oppressive taxes upon industry.[56]

Opposed to these ideas, which were politically adopted by the Liberal Republicans, the regular Republicans insisted upon the necessity of maintaining control of the politics of the Southern states in order to protect migrating capital and people. Social ostracism and personal violence, said President Grant in his message of 1871, prevented "immigration and the flow of much-needed capital into the States lately in rebellion."[57] The South, echoed the New York *Times* in the midst of the campaign, needed local governments which would protect citizens. Only the Republican party could assume solid achievement and national prosperity and "restrain with firmness any resistance to the new order of things." The South had always depended upon outside capital, and the war had destroyed whatever accumulation might have existed. "Industry is sluggish, trade creeps from point to point, manufactures are feeble and few," cried the administration journal as it demanded a continuation of the policy which held out "every encouragement . . . to Northern and foreign capitalists."[58] As the campaign went on Greeley's *Tribune* carried more items concerning available Southern farm lands and showed that "had it not been for carpetbag mismanagement, this country today would be filled with millions of Northern or foreign yeomanry carving out farms, or working in . . . iron, copper, coal, and

[56] *Ibid.,* September 4, 1871.
[57] J. D. Richardson (ed.), *Messages and Papers of the Presidents* (Washington, 1898), VII, 153.
[58] New York *Times,* May 24, 28, 1872.

marble."[59] At the same time, Secretary Boutwell went into North Carolina to sing the praises of the carpetbaggers and assure the North Carolinians that neither immigrants nor capital could be safe in Democratic regions.[60] "The business men of the South," wrote a carpetbagger to the Republican national committee, "want stability in business, which the election of Greeley . . . will not insure."[61]

Although other factors combined to prevent Greeley's election, his Southern program had made considerable impression on the voters. The carpetbaggers had received much unfavorable publicity during the campaign, and the idea that the friction between the races in the South was caused by dishonest adventurers, who drove out industry, was widely spread over the North.[62] In the next few years the horrors of carpetbaggery were to be proclaimed by the "liberal" and Democratic press until the masters of capital were convinced that only the removal of this "swarm of locusts" would make possible the economic exploitation of the section.

At the close of the election, Greeley sadly turned to advise the Southerners to accept the situation and "set to work to build up their section's industrial and commercial prosperity." This advice, said the defeated candidate, would sound harsh to men who were unable to pay the enormous taxes imposed by the carpetbaggers.[63] How little encouragement the South might receive from the government in such an effort was evident from the attitude of the administration press. The New York *Times* ridiculed Greeley's efforts to

---

[59] New York *Tribune*, July 11, 1872.
[60] *Ibid.*, July 18, 1872.
[61] B. F. Whittemore to W. E. Chandler, July 22, 1872, W. E. Chandler MSS. (in Library of Congress).
[62] New York *Tribune*, September 28, 1872.
[63] *Ibid.*, November 13, 1872.

advise his supporters, and the administration organ in Washington announced that the South was responsible for any misfortunes which had come upon it. Acceptance of Republicanism, the paper implied, was the only hope for the section.[64]

The country had not long to wait for the development of the Republican policy in the South. Following immediately upon the election, there ensued a struggle between two groups of carpetbaggers for the control of Louisiana.[65] Although President Grant attempted to remain impartial between the contending factions,[66] the New York *Tribune,* continuing its rôle as the Bible of the industrialists, lost no opportunity to point out the intimate connection between Republican policies and the disordered commonwealth. It spoke feelingly about the "plundered community," showed that its government was founded upon fraud, and declared that the dispute "prostitutes the business of the State." Louisiana finances were kept before the eye of the northern people, and the "moneyed interests of the country" were warned against investments in a state whose governor could sell its railroad interests without consulting the legislature and which had a debt of twenty-four millions.[67]

At the same time that Louisiana was troubling the political waters, other points of the South were contributing testimony to the economic derangements attendant upon carpetbag governments. In Arkansas there were quarrels

---

[64] New York *Times,* November 14, 1872; *National Intelligencer,* November 11, 1872.

[65] William A. Dunning, *Reconstruction, Economic and Political* (New York, 1907), 217.

[66] Grant to W. W. Belknap, January 5, 1873, Grant MSS. Letter Book (in Library of Congress).

[67] New York *Tribune,* January 4, March 1, February 24, 26, June 9, July 28, October 15, 1873; January 6, 1874.

between factions of the Republican party comparable to those in Louisiana, while the debts and taxes of the state were rising.[68] The *Tribune* published a traveler's account of the corruption and the absurdities of the "prostrate State" of South Carolina where a handful of unscrupulous whites controlled the Negro legislature.[69] If anything were needed to impress the lesson it was furnished by the condition in the District of Columbia. At the beginning of Reconstruction, Congress had granted the suffrage to the Negroes of the District. Designed as an experiment to show the capacity of the Negro for citizenship, it soon showed the reverse. Under "Boss" Shepherd's direction the Negroes voted for new bond issues and went to the polls to approve the valiant plans which the District governor was making to pull the capital city out of the mud. But the property holders and taxpayers of the District, outvoted by the Negroes, ignored the improvements to gaze with horrible forebodings upon the mounting debt.[70] This was sufficiently close to the Northern voter and taxpayer to clarify his view on the Radical program in the South. Perhaps an underlying fear, which few dared to express, was the danger which was involved in the rising movement of the lower classes throughout the country. The Granger movement in the West was assailing the citadels of private monopoly, and there was a conceivable connection between these elements and the "bottom rails" who had gotten on top in the South. Two years before one observer had noticed that there were six thousand native adult whites in Georgia "who cannot read or write, and if to them were added the whole bulk of the negro population, so vast a mass of ignorance would be found that, if

---

[68] *Ibid.*, May 19, June 4, 1873.
[69] *Ibid.*, April 8, 19, 1873.
[70] *Ibid.*, April 17, 19, May 10, 1873; *National Intelligencer*, February 13, 1873. See also New York *Times*, December 4, 1872.

combined for any political purpose it would sweep away all opposition the intelligent class might make. Many thoughtful men are apprehensive that the ignorant voters will, in the future, form a party by themselves as dangerous to the interests of society as the communists of France."[71]

Evidence of a growing reaction in the North came simultaneously with these troubles in the South. In May, 1873, Senator Matt Carpenter, long a supporter of the extreme Radical position, visited Louisiana with a congressional committee. To the people of New Orleans the Wisconsin senator promised a better government and urged that they turn their attention from politics to trade and business.[72] Eugene Hale, a member of Congress from Maine, presiding over his state's Republican convention, announced that he was "tired and sick of some of the carpet-bag governments."[73] Generally, men were coming to the belief that the poverty of the Southern states was due to the villainies of the carpetbaggers, and they were coming to perceive that this had a national significance. The "withdrawal of taxes, which the Southern States might pay under favorable circumstances, throws just that additional burden upon the tax-paying property of the North," announced the *Tribune*.[74] Even George F. Hoar came to admit that the character of the carpetbaggers was such that they would not have been tolerated in the North.[75]

With the development of a sentiment of opposition to the carpetbaggers, there came a new hope that a change of policy might throw the South open for migration of capital

---

[71] New York *Tribune,* June 21, 1871.
[72] *Ibid.,* May 24, 1873.
[73] *Ibid.,* June 21, 1873.
[74] *Ibid.,* August 15, 1873.
[75] George F. Hoar, *Autobiography of Seventy Years* (New York, 1903), II, 160–61.

and for manufacturing. Surveying the situation, it was noticed that only South Carolina and Louisiana were still in 1873 oppressed by excessive taxes, while the other states might welcome Northern mills and factories. Virginia, for example, had accepted Reconstruction, avoided carpetbaggers, and proceeded forward steadily in industrial development. The lesson was obvious—if the government abandoned its policy of upholding carpetbaggers, prosperity would come to the South. Propositions for moving New England cotton mills to the South were reported and discussed in the press and on the floors of Congress. Even Southerners took a new hope from the renewed discussion of capital moving South.[76]

Standing in the way of a change of policy stood the fact that stories of Southern outrages had been the stock in trade of the Radicals since 1866, and the politicians had no thought of abandoning so profitable a source of political ammunition. But even the "outrage business" received a death blow in the congressional campaign of 1874. In the midst of the campaign an Alabama congressman published a list of murders and acts of violence which had recently taken place in his state. Long suspicious of such stories, the New York *Tribune* immediately investigated and found no substantial basis for the congressman's charges.[77] Thereafter the accumulating atrocity stories were received dubiously by the Northern people. However, the Southern carpetbaggers were merely goaded into action by this exposure, and a hastily called convention of Republican politicians assembled in Chattanooga to prepare an authentic list of atrocities for the benefit of the Northern voter and to convince Con-

---

[76] New York *Tribune*, September 22, December 24, 1873; January 7, 17, 22, February 16, July 31, 1874.
[77] *Ibid.*, September 1, October 7, 12, 1874.

gress that further protection should be given at elections. But the convention proved abortive. While a number of the delegates came prepared to contribute atrocity stories and demand more federal interference, a larger number were found to have come to prevent a "new flood of misrepresentations" which would "frighten men and capital from their neglected fields and factories." This latter class was composed of men who had become identified with the material interests of the South. Delegates from North Carolina were ready to declare that they had not heard of a political assault in their state for more than a year. The convention appointed a committee on "Facts and Statistics" which never reported, and passed general resolutions asserting that violence toward loyal men was common, but the total effect of the meeting was to give the South a clean bill of health.[78] With the "outrage" business played out, the Republicans were deprived of their leading arguments for continuing in power, while the Democrats and the Liberal Republicans insisted that business was injured by the plundering governments of the Southern states. Testimony was sedulously gathered by the *Tribune* to show that there were no outrages in Tennessee or Kentucky and that migrating capital was safe in those states.[79]

The eventual victory of those who preferred the economic to the political exploitation of the South was foreshadowed in the election returns. The Democrats won control of Congress, and Republican politicians turned to a new stock taking. "We have got a hard lot from the South," said Postmaster-General Marshall Jewell as he surveyed the carpetbag governments, "and the people will not submit to it any longer, nor do I blame them."[80] To Jewell's mind the car-

---

[78] *Ibid.,* October 14, 15, 21, 1874.
[79] *Ibid.,* October 24, November 3, 1874.
[80] Jewell to E. B. Washburne, December 5, 1874, Washburne MSS.

petbaggers did not have "among them one really first class man."[81] A consul in Germany thought it "too d—d bad that our party should be ruined and have to go to the wall through the careless labors of such cattle" as the Louisiana carpetbaggers. But, said this observer, the people were "tired out with this wornout cry of 'Southern Outrages!!!' Hard times and heavy taxes make them wish the 'nigger' 'everlasting nigger' were in —— or Africa. . . . It is amazing the change that has taken place in the last two years in public sentiment."[82] Even Vice-President Wilson concluded that the Republican party would have to change its policy. He noticed, after a trip through the South, that business conditions had improved and a spirit of industry was spreading among the Southern whites.[83] Wisconsin's Senator Howe ruefully regarded the wreck of Republican hopes and suddenly remembered that the war was not "fought for the 'nigger' " and the Negro was not "the end and aim of all our effort."[84]

The congressional elections of 1874 marked the abandonment of political Reconstruction by the Northern voters. The repudiated Radicals continued their course until after they had delivered the presidency to Hayes, but the popular vote in the North was cast in 1876 for Tilden and for a different method of exploiting the South. With the withdrawal of the Federal troops from the South, the masters of capital embarked upon a policy of conciliating their former enemies and of slow infiltration into their conquered but stubborn provinces.

A single glimpse at the situation a decade later will suffice to illustrate the new technique which the North came to

---

[81] Jewell to Lucius Fairchild, December 28, 1874, Fairchild MSS.
[82] T. Wilson to Fairchild, January 17, 1875, Fairchild MSS.
[83] New York *Tribune,* June 5, 1875.
[84] T. O. Howe to Fairchild, June 14, 1875, Fairchild MSS.

employ in dealing with the South. In 1885 young William McKinley went to plead with the people of Virginia to send a protectionist to the Senate. "Do you imagine that anybody is coming to Virginia with his money to build a mill, or a factory, or a furnace, and develop your coal and your ore, bring his money down here, when you vote every time against his interests. . . .?" he asked. "If you think so, you might just as well be undeceived now, for they will not come. . . . Be assured that the Republicans of the North harbor no resentments—only ask for the results of the war. They wish you the highest prosperity and the greatest development."[85] The change from the method of coercion to that of appeal was great, but the hope was still alive that in spite of the abandonment of political Reconstruction the South would receive the master of capital with his promises of prosperity.

---

[85] William McKinley, *Speeches and Addresses* (New York, 1893), 181–95.

FIVE

Some New Aspects of the Proslavery Argument

A MONG the accepted truisms of Southern History is the contention that the rise of the abolition movement in the North caused the South to turn to the defense of slavery. In the midst of the sectional controversy, Southerners constantly asserted that their own insistence upon the validity of slavery was due to abolition agitation. In 1843, George Tucker proclaimed that "the efforts of Abolitionists have hitherto made the people in the slaveholding states cling to it [slavery] more tenaciously. Those efforts are viewed by them as an intermeddling in their domestic concerns that is equally unwarranted by the comity that is due to sister states, and to the solemn pledges of the Federal compact."[1] This view has continued to be accepted, with even such critical historians as Charles and Mary Beard declaring that "the immediate effect of the anti-slavery clangor

---

Read before the twentieth anniversary celebration of the Association for the Study of Negro Life and History, Chicago, September 10, 1935. Reprinted by permission from the *Journal of Negro History*, 21: 1–14 (January, 1936).
[1] George Tucker, *Progress of the United States in Population and Wealth* (Richmond, 1843), 108.

was a consolidation of forces and a searching of minds and hearts for an effective answer. Clearly the hour for apologetics had arrived and human intelligence was equal to the occasion."[2]

Despite such unanimity of testimony, the assertion that the proslavery argument was an answer to abolitionism will not stand the light of examination. A cursory glance at Southern polemics before Garrison will suffice to show that all of the features of the proslavery argument were already in circulation before the Garrisonian crusade was launched, while an examination of the situation in the South in the period before the fiery *Libertor* came to shock the planter's sensibilities will indicate that the movement grew out of definitely Southern conditions and that if Garrison had never lived it would have been desirable for the Southern planters to have invented him.

Textually, the proslavery argument developed with the spread of slavery on the American continent. The first chapter of the argument was written when slaves were introduced to the American colonists. Unknown to English law and practice, slavery needed a rationalization for its existence. Among a peole whose ideology and idiom was that of the church and the Bible, it was but natural that the explanation of a new labor system should be couched in the language of Christianity. Slavery was a blessing to the African because as a result he was brought into contact with Christianity and given the hope of eternal salvation. Throughout the colonial period the conversion of slaves was advocated in royal instructions to colonial governors and sought through the activities of the Anglican clergy. Pious pirates who could plunder the Spanish Main in be-

---

[2] Charles A. and Mary Beard, *Rise of American Civilization* (New York, 1927), I, 703.

half of Protestantism need have no scruple against bringing black savages from pagan darkness to the portals of paradise. The defense of the traffic in the name of missionary zeal was as old as the slave trade, and far antedated Garrisonian abolitionism.[3]

The second chapter of the proslavery argument developed out of a situation quite similar to that which finally called for the complete formulation of the Southern viewpoint. For three-quarters of a century after the establishment of Jamestown, the English settlers in the new world failed in their Christian duty to purchase the ebony cargoes of the mercantile missionaries of the slave trade. During that period, the labor supply of Virginia and Maryland was furnished by indentured servants from England and the continent. In those years, the first settlers and those possessed of native shrewdness or political influence obtained the best lands of the river bottoms and began to develop the plantation system. Indentured servants, at the end of their indentures, were forced into the back country where poorer soil and the inaccessibility of their lands made them easily exploited by the nascent planter aristocracy, who, through Governor Berkeley and the council, were able to dominate Virginia society. The control of these tidewater planters, however, was frequently threatened by the grumblings of the restive people of the back country. With their control endangered by these exploited people, the planters took steps to prevent the addition of more discordant elements to the colony's population. In 1670, the colonial assembly passed an act forbidding the importation of criminals—

---

[3] J. C. Hurd, *Laws of Freedom and Bondage* (Boston, 1858), I, 160–163; M. W. Jernegan, *Laboring and Dependent Classes in Colonial America, 1607–1783* (Chicago, 1931), 27–31; cf. also, John Fiske, *Old Virginia and Her Neighbors* (Boston, 1897), I, 15–16.

"felons and other desperate villains"—into the colony.[4] But
the measure was too late. Six years later came the movement
which the planters had dreaded. Bacon's rebellion almost
destroyed the planter aristocracy and confirmed their worst
fears of the indentured servant. To escape the menace of
the lower classes, the planters had recourse to the slave
traders, and soon the African had supplanted the European
in the tobacco fields of Virginia. In addition to the obvious
advantages of a servant who would not become a competi-
tor, and would not demand political rights, the planters
found the Negroes cheaper. The superiority of Negro over
white labor from the standpoint of social control and the
economic advantages of a workman who could serve for life
were added to Christian duty as arguments for slavery.[5]

A third element was added to the apologetics for slavery
with the establishment of the colonies of South Carolina
and Georgia. South Carolina was established by planters
from Bermuda who brought with them both slavery and
the plantation system. Georgia, however, was established
without slaves, but it was not long before Oglethorpe's ambitious colonists were petitioning the trustees to abandon
their scruples and permit large landholdings and the introduction of slave labor. In addition to the economy of slavery, which they urged, the distinctive contribution of
Georgia and South Carolina to the growing rationale of
slavery was the contention that only Negroes could with-
stand the heat and moisture of the Southern climate.[6]

---

[4] W. W. Henning, *Statutes of Virginia, II,* 509–10.

[5] J. T. Adams, *Provincial Society* (New York, 1927), 104, 196–197;
Leonidas Dodson, *Alexander Spottswood, Governor of Colonial
Virginia, 1710–1722* (Philadelphia, 1932), 46.

[6] H. B. Fant, "The Labor Policy of the Trustees for Establishing
the Colony of Georgia in America," *Georgia Historical Quarterly,*
XVI, 1–16; and David M. Potter, "The Rise of the Plantation System in Georgia," *ibid.,* 114–135.

About the time that Georgia was learning the desirability of slave labor from experience, a change was under way in Virginia. Historians, following the lead of Southern writers, have made much of the fact that the revolutionary generation of Virginians was opposed to slavery. The leaders of this period, however, were not drawn from the old tidewater section, but were identified with the western parts of the state, or represented the back country. After Bacon's rebellion ended in defeat, the back country people were leaderless until the Scotch-Irish and Germans filled up the piedmont and valley sections of the state. Almost simultaneously, the Great Awakening spread among the people of the back country and the frontier. The revival was more than a religious movement, and resulted in giving both organization and leadership to the poorer classes.[7] In conjunction with the Scotch-Irish, these elements were able to challenge the control of the planter aristocracy. Under the leadership of Patrick Henry and Thomas Jefferson the planters were forced to take a subordinate position, while the western and radical elements took Virginia into the Revolutionary War. Part of the reason for the victory of these classes was the declining price of tobacco and of slaves.

Although Virginians fell under the influence of the back country to the extent that enthusiasm for slavery suffered a momentary decline, the equalitarian sentiments of the Declaration of Independence made no appeal to the planters of South Carolina and Georgia. These states entered the Revolution, but they brought no adherence to the democratic theories upon which the struggle was based. Instead, they continually advocated slavery and in the Constitutional

---

[7] W. M. Gewehr, *The Great Awakening in Virginia* (Durham, N. C., 1930), 187ff.; cf. T. M. Whitfield, *Slavery Agitation in Virginia, 1829–1832* (Baltimore, 1930), 3–4.

convention they forced a compromise which would perpetu-
ate the institution. Not only did the South Carolinians support slavery on the grounds of property rights, but Pierce
Butler, speaking in the convention, declared that slavery
was a positive benefit to the nation since the labor of a slave
was as much a contribution to the national wealth as that
of a freeman. Rutledge of South Carolina further alleged
that the New England shippers were benefited by the slave
trade. In general, the delegates from the lower South insisted that since slavery benefited one portion of the country
it must be protected by the Federal government.[8]

This attitude of the South Carolinians soon received another expression with the opening of the first Congress.
When Pennsylvania Quakers petitioned Congress for the
end of slavery, Jackson of Georgia rose to ask "if the whole
morality of the world is confined to the Quakers?" The
Saviour, he proclaimed, had permitted slavery. South Carolina's Tucker added to the discussion by pointing out that
slavery was Biblically sound. In the discussion which followed, various members of the South Carolina and Georgia
delegations justified slavery on Biblical, historical, and
humanitarian grounds. So thoroughly did they canvass the
situation that writers in the post-Garrison period were only
able to add details and elaborations to these early exposi-
tions. The proslavery argument, in its full outlines, was at
least as old as the Congress of the United States.[9]

From the time of this debate in Congress the central point
of interest in the development of the proslavery argument
is not concerned with its textual development but with its

---

[8] Henry Wilson, *Rise and Fall of the Slave Power* (Boston, 1872–
77), I, 43–44, 49–50.
[9] T. H. Benton, *Abridgment of the Debates of Congress,* I, 208ff.;
Henry Wilson, *op. cit.,* I, 61–67.

spread until it finally received the intellectual assent of the great majority of the Southerners. Fundamentally, the argument, with its exhausting excursion into Biblical exegesis, its search for historical incidents to prove that slavery was the natural lot of man, its comparison of the benefits of bondage with the hazards of freedom, and its glorification of agrarian economics and a patriarchal society became a system of metaphysics which constituted the whole philosophy of Southern life.

Two major factors in the period from the first Quaker petitions in Congress to the publication of Garrison's *Liberator* account for the development and spread of the proslavery argument. The first of these was the intensification of social stratification in the South after the invention of the cotton gin, and the second was the growth of sectional rivalry within the United States. Both contributed to the necessity for formulating the philosophic concepts upon which plantation society was based.

The immediate effect of the invention of the cotton gin was to increase the value of the slaves which were held in the states of the upper South. Whereas slavery had been regarded for some years as an unprofitable institution, the demand for laborers in the cotton fields soon raised their value and gave to the planters of Virginia a definite economic motive for the preservation and spread of slavery. In addition, it enabled the planter class, through their wealth, to again dominate the government and the social life of their states. The widening gulf between the social classes brought divergence of views on slavery. While the men of the western counties and of the back country continued to adhere to the democratic philosophy of the Revolution, the tidewater slaveholders adopted the more comfortable doctrines of the South Carolinians. In 1807 Representative Early told his colleagues in Congress that

"Southern people do not regard this trade as a crime. They are all concerned in slavery. . . . If they considered it a crime they would necessarily accuse themselves. I will tell the truth. A large majority of them do not consider it even an evil."[10] Two years later the Pennsylvania Society for Promoting the Abolition of Slavery noted that in the South "hitherto the approving voice of the community and the liberal interpretation of the laws have smoothed the path of duty and promoted a satisfactory issue to our own humane exertions. At present, the sentiments of our fellow citizens and the decisions of our courts are less auspicious."[11]

At the same time that the tidewater aristocracy were turning to the defense of slavery, the western sections of the South were giving vent to an increasing restlessness. In Virginia the constitution of 1776 had given the western sections a lesser representation, and while the westerners paid a greater share of the taxes of the state, they received less from the government than the east. The need of the western sections for internal improvements was ignored by the east, while property qualifications for the suffrage bore harder on the piedmont and valley than on the tidewater. Demands for reform were frequent, and Virginia's western counties insisted for two decades on a constitutional convention which would equalize the burdens and benefits of government. As part of this sectional and social strife in Virginia, the westerners launched an attack upon the slave property of the tidewater planters.[12]

In the rest of the South similar situations existed. Along

---

[10] Wilson, *op. cit.*, I, 85.

[11] Edward Needles, *An Historical Memoir of the Pennsylvania Society for Promoting the Abolition of Slavery* (Philadelphia, 1848), 56.

[12] Charles H. Ambler, "History of West Virginia," *American Historical Review*, XV, 764.

the frontier region opposition to the aristocracy and a pro-
test against slavery went hand in hand. In East Tennessee
abolition journalism began, and within a few years Benjamin Lundy traveled the mountain regions of Tennessee and
North Carolina organizing antislavery societies among the
lowly. Antislavery societies made their appearance in Kentucky in 1808, in Tennessee in 1814, in North Carolina in
1816, Maryland in 1817, and in Virginia in 1823. Of the
one hundred and thirty abolition societies in the country in
1827, one hundred and six were in the western parts of the
Southern states. Among the Methodist, Presbyterian and
Baptist churches, whose membership was especially strong
in the western sections, there was a widespread opposition
to an institution which was, according to the Presbyterian
general assembly of 1818, "a gross violation of the most
precious and moral rights of human nature, as utterly in-
consistent with the law of God . . . and as totally irrecon-
cilable with the spirit and principles of the gospel of
Christ."[13] By the close of the 1820's there was a definite
alignment of western antislavery elements against the tidewater slaveholders.[14]

Serious though this division of classes was to the slave-
holder, it was complicated by the fact that in the years after
Jefferson's assumption of the Presidency there was an increasing rivalry between the North and the South for the
control of the government. In 1803 New England opposed
the purchase of Louisiana, partly on the grounds that it
would give a new area in which slavery could expand. In
the following years, the New Englanders opposed the Southern and Western war of 1812, and demanded a tariff which
was anathema to the Southerners. In 1820, the Missouri

---

[13] A. B. Hart, *Slavery and Abolition* (New York, 1916), 160–161.
[14] *Life, Travels and Opinions of Benjamin Lundy*, by his children
(Philadelphia, 1847), 218.

Compromise gave further evidence of the opposition of the North to the expansion of Southern institutions. In this situation the planters faced the danger of an alliance of the North with the West either under the formula of Clay's American System or under the leveling enthusiasms of Jacksonian Democracy. With such alliance against them the Lords of the Manor would be ruined both economically and socially.

Faced with the necessity of protecting both their property and their social and political control, the slaveholders strove to obtain unity within their section. Two methods of action developed through the years. The one was a vicious attack upon the North and especially the New Englanders, and the other was the proslavery argument. Through the first, the planter class appealed to the provincialism of their poorer neighbors, and through the second they attempted to substitute the sense of racial superiority for the mounting class consciousness of the nonslaveholders.

In order to accomplish the first of these objects, the Southern leaders lost no opportunity to place the onus of the sectional controversy upon the alien Yankee. After the Missouri Compromise an increasing "irritability" on the part of the Southerners in Congress was noted, and antislavery writings were frequently denounced. The South, asserted South Carolina's Congressman Drayton in 1828, would "rather endure all the calamities of civil war . . . than parley for an instant upon the right of any power than our own to interfere with the regulation of our slaves."[15] Observers from the North noted the Southern jealousy of the North, and the editor of the *New England Review* called attention to the "abuse heaped by Southern demagogues

---

[15] W. H. Smith, *A Political History of Slavery* (New York, 1903), I, 25–35.

upon New England."[16] But perhaps the best of the sectional diatribes of the preGarrison period was the product of the pen of Robert James Turnbull of South Carolina. Writing under the name of "Brutus," he deplored the tendency of Northern state legislatures to "pour forth the phials of their wrath" against the "Fundamental Polity" of the Southern States. "Domestic servitude is so intimately interwoven with our prosperity," declared "Brutus," "that to talk of its abolition is to speak of writing us out of our civil and political existence."[17] It is evident from the attitude which the slaveholders were taking that Garrison's announcement of his uncompromising hostility to slavery played directly into the hands of those who would attribute the attack on slavery to outside interference. In truth, the exact opposite of this generally accepted idea may be true. It is conceivable that the Southern determination to defend slavery by an attack upon the North may have caused antislavery men to despair of gradual emancipation and join with Garrison in a demand for immediate and uncompensated abolition!

Appeals to local patriotism, however, were but part of the tactics of the planters. More significant were the efforts made to obtain unity of sentiment among all classes. Violence and coercion played its part in this movement, while public meetings attempted to whip up the semblance of coöperation. In Virginia when a Norfolk lawyer denounced slavery in a newspaper article he was accused of wanting to produce another Santo Domingo and a meeting appointed a committee to report on the state of the local police. In 1827 an antislavery meeting in Smithfield, Virginia, was stopped on the grounds that the law did not

[16] Alice Adams, *The Neglected Period of Anti-Slavery in America, 1808–1831* (Boston, 1908), 113ff.
[17] William Jay, *Miscellaneous Writings on Slavery* (Boston, 1853); Alice Adams, *op. cit.*, 117.

specifically permit meetings for such a purpose.[18] In 1825 a young South Carolinian canceled his subscription to the *Genius of Universal Emancipation* on the grounds that neither his health nor the successful prosecution of his profession would permit him to receive so dangerous a publication.[19]

That the planters were afraid of the common people of the South is borne out by a pamphlet by Z. Kingsley, a native of Florida. Agriculture, said Kingsley, was the foundation of Southern life, and agriculture was dependent upon the "perpetuation of that kind of labor which now produces it and which seems best adapted, under all circumstances, to render it profitable to the Southern Capitalist." To Kingsley's mind, the slaves, in addition to being happier, were "equally virtuous, moral, and less corrupted than the ordinary class of laboring whites." Moreover, Negroes were more productive than whites, and "under a just and prudent system of management, Negroes are safe, permanent, productive and growing property, and easily governed; that they are sober, discreet, honest and obliging, are less troublesome, and possess a much better moral character than the ordinary class of corrupted whites of similar condition." In carrying out his argument, the Floridan laid the foundation for the later work of Fitzhugh by declaring that "slavery is a necessary state of control from which no condition of society can be perfectly free. The term is applicable to, and fits all grades and conditions in almost every point of view, whether moral, physical, or political."[20]

Despite this attitude toward the lower classes, the planters

---

[18] Adams, *op. cit.*, 112.
[19] *Genius of Universal Emancipation*, 6, 61.
[20] Z. Kingsley, *A Treatise on the Patriarchal, or Co-operative System of Society. . . . With its Necessity and Advantages* (n. p., second edition, 1829).

were obliged to appeal to them in the proslavery argument. The primary purpose of this exposition was to convince the non-slaveholding whites of the superiority of white over Negro blood. An analysis of the literature of the Southern "defense" will indicate that the fundamental premise of the slaveholders was that Negroes were inferior to whites. Throughout the era of the sectional conflict ministers of the Southern churches searched the Scriptures and compared Hebrew texts to show that God had made the Negroes a subordinate race and ordained them for slavery. In addition, a pseudo-anthropology demonstrated the biological inferiority of the Negro race. In the field of politics, the planters abandoned the principles of democracy, and frankly proclaimed that the Declaration of Independence was designed for white men alone.

Aiding in the process of convincing the non-slaveholders of the desirability of slavery was the economic situation in the South before 1830. The opening up of great regions in the Southwest, suitable for the growing of cotton and the establishment of the plantation system, made it possible for the poorer classes to migrate to the new lands and become planters. The possibility of joining the ranks of the aristocracy was sufficient to lead yeomen and poor whites to accept the philosophy of the planters before they had obtained the wealth necessary for admission into the charmed society of the Lords of the Manor. In 1828–1829 the western counties of Virginia, after forcing the calling of a constitutional convention, accepted a compromise on representation and dropped their opposition to slavery because they expected western Virginia to become wealthy and its inhabitants slaveholders.[21] At the same time, the situation in

---

[21] C. H. Ambler, *History of West Virginia* (New York, 1933), 221ff.

Santo Domingo and occasional slave insurrections in the South seemed to confirm the planters' thesis of a fundamental hostility between the races and to render slavery necessary as an institution of social control. After the debates in the Virginia legislature following the Southampton massacre the opposition to slavery disappeared in Virginia and the people accepted the philosophy which Professor Dew came forth to expound. William and Mary College in Virginia and the College of Charleston took over the congenial task of educating the young men of the back country and the up country to the ideals of the aristocracy, and the churches which had formerly denounced slavery now gave divine sanction to the institution. So thoroughly did the whites of the South become imbued with the ideal of white supremacy that a recent writer could find ample evidence to substantiate a thesis that the maintenance of white supremacy has been the "central theme of Southern history."[22]

But despite the testimony from poor whites, overseers, and the lesser yeomanry which Professor Phillips marshalled to support his thesis, the real central theme of Southern history seems to have been the maintenance of the planter class in control. The proslavery argument carried but little promise to the lower classes, yet it sufficed to draw a line of demarkation between the exploited groups of the South. Playing upon the race prejudice which the argument inculcated, the planter aristocrat and his Bourbon successor have been able to remain in control. When the Civil War began, the non-slaveholders of the South did battle to maintain the Southern system of life. Following the war, there was imminent danger that the lower orders might forget race and unite, but the Ku Klux Klan saved the day for the Bourbons.

---

[22] U. B. Phillips, "The Central Theme of Southern History," *American Historical Review* XXXIV (October, 1928), 30–43.

In the nineties, the Populist movement brought whites and blacks of the oppressed classes together, but again the heritage of the proslavery argument brought division and eventuated in new constitutions which effectually disfranchised both the Negroes and their potential allies among the poor whites. Occasional lynchings have sufficed to keep burning the flames first kindled by the proslavery argument. Only in recent months has depression-born necessity brought tenant farmers of both races to stand shoulder to shoulder against their oppressors. For more than a century, the proslavery argument has enabled the planting aristocrats to dominate Southern society.

SIX

The Pryor-Potter Duel

T HE second World War, like the first, has given birth to
numerous proposals for a world-wide political organization which might possess the necessary power and influence
to insure peace. Proponents of schemes of unity have repeatedly pointed to the example of the United States, where
thirteen revolting colonies, faced by a common enemy, laid
aside their differences to form a new nation. If, say the advo-
cates of a world federation, the American colonies could
form a successful union, the nations of the world might like-
wise unite to promote the general welfare, establish justice,
and secure the blessings of liberty to all mankind.

Such flaccid analogy begins with the easy assumption that
the simple machinery for interstate communion was the
primary force in holding the American states in the federal
union. It ignores the fact that the will to unite preceded the
act of unification, and it forgets that the Union was broken
when the spirit of coöperation succumbed before conflicting
sectional interests. It was psychology, not political machinery, that united the United States, and it was the spirit

Read before the State Historical Society of Wisconsin at Milwaukee on September 16, 1943. Reprinted by permission from the
Wisconsin Magazine of History, 27: 400–409 (September, 1943).

of compromise and conciliation that enabled the denizens of diverse regions, with different and often conflicting economic interests, intellectual backgrounds, and social organizations to work and live together in a common country.

The essential element in the American system was the capacity for compromise. However violently men of different opinions, classes, or areas disagreed, they possessed a common willingness to resolve their differences by mutual concessions. The compromises of the Constitution became, in truth, symbols of the American way of life, and in the dramatic crises of 1820, 1833, and 1850, there was always a Henry Clay ready to offer a verbal formula under which contending forces could come to agreement. Such great formal compromises were paralleled by hundreds of minor ones. Every law passed by Congress, and every platform of a political party, was the product of compromises, of concessions, and of conciliation. "We are all Republicans, we are all Federalists," said Thomas Jefferson as he applied cooling words of wisdom to brows grown feverish in partisan rancor.

This was the American system: this the American spirit. It was the spirit which prevailed from the day when Patrick Henry proclaimed that he was no longer a Virginian but an American until that other day when Abraham Lincoln gazed wistfully towards the right bank of the Potomac pleading with the Southerners: "We are not enemies, but friends. We must not be enemies."

But Abraham Lincoln pleaded in vain. Though he might hope that better angels would touch "the mystic chords of memory," he knew that the American spirit had changed. The will to compromise was gone, and the Civil War came because men had lost the spirit of conciliation and concession. The machinery of the Union crumbled quickly when its psychological foundations gave way.

Long before 1861 signs and portents of the coming catastrophe multiplied. In the years just before Fort Sumter every event, however innocent its origin, was twisted into significance for the sectional conflict. The peaceful migration of homeseekers to new territory became a deep-laid plot to steal a new state for slavery or for freedom. The rough brawls of a frontier community grew in the telling into mighty conflicts between the armed forces of righteousness and darkness. Poor, demented John Brown hatched a silly plot in his tortured mind, struck a madman's blind blow at slavery, and the sovereign state of Virginia, with never a suggestion that he be treated as a lunatic, solemnly hanged him for treason. In such an atmosphere, events lost their true meaning and took on implications which transcended reason.

One such event, symptomatic of this whole era, was the near-duel between Virginia's Roger Pryor and Wisconsin's John F. Potter. In calmer times, the undignified wrangle between these two congressmen might have been dismissed as indecorous or ridiculous behavior. But the April of 1860 was not calm: the Democratic Convention met within a week, and the Republicans assembled exactly a month after the conclusion of the Pryor-Potter affair. The very air of Washington was electric with emotion, and the Pryor-Potter duel, unimportant in itself, was a symbol of the disparate attitudes of the two sections of a once-united country.

The participants in this fiasco were each representative of the majority attitude in their respective sections. Roger Pryor, not quite thirty-two years of age, was tall and straight, with elastic step and physical vigor. He was a fiery, impassioned speaker with a reputation as a convincing orator. Descended from the First Families of Virginia, educated at Hampden-Sydney College and the University of Virginia, he had already made a mark for himself as an ardent fire-eating Southerner. Combining law with journalism, he had practiced at the Virginia bar, had founded two transitory pro-Southern newspapers, and had gained repute as a forthright editor. He had won, as well, notoriety as a duelist, backing up his editorial opinions with pistol and sword in several encounters. In 1858 he had attended the Southern Commercial Convention at Montgomery and had there led the forces which opposed reopening the African slave trade. But, though he might have opposed this move, no member of the Southern fire-eating group was more extreme than he in urging the South to break both the economic and the political shackles which bound her to the North. In 1859 Virginia sent him to the House of Representatives, and in his first session he assumed a leading position in debates with the Northerners. Frequently in his speeches he alluded to his career as a duelist and expressed his willingness to meet his Yankee antagonists on the field of honor.[1]

John Fox Potter sprang from a different background and partook of a different tradition. A native of Maine, he attended Phillips Academy at Exeter, and in 1838, aged twenty-one, he migrated to frontier Wisconsin. Here he took up land and quickly combined the trades of farmer, lawyer, and politician. From 1842 to 1846 he served as a judge in Walworth County, and for some years he was active, in a minor way, in the Whig and Free-Soil parties. Unknown to fame, he was known to his neighbors as a man of some culture, with a sense of humor, and a genial and companionable disposition. He was charitable, kind to animals, and not addicted to the belligerency which characterized his career in Congress. Legend has it—and the legend emerged much later—that on one occasion, shortly after his arrival in Wis-

---

[1] *Dictionary of American Biography,* 15: 256; Madison *Democrat,* March 18, 1919; New York *Tribune,* April 16, 1860. Cf. also Avery Craven, *The Coming of the Civil War* (New York, 1942), 399.

consin, he was walking along a narrow path when he saw an Indian raise his rifle and carefully aim at his breast. But Potter was fearless: his steady gaze into the Indian's eye forced the treacherous savage to lower the firearm and vanish into the wilderness![2]

In 1856, not because of this unsuspected fearlessness, but because of his genial character, his well-known antislavery views, and his political services, his neighbors of East Troy sent John Potter to the State Assembly. The most important legislation of this session was the scandalous land grant to the La Crosse and Milwaukee Railroad Company. John F. Potter introduced the bill in the assembly. But, although the railroad distributed nearly $900,000 worth of stocks and bonds to legislators and state officials in return for the grant, Potter received no monetary reward for his conspicuous services.[3] Nevertheless, hostile Democrats asserted that Potter was as guilty as the bribe-taking legislators: he had "begged for days" to be allowed to introduce the bill, and his reward was election to the Congress of the United States.[4]

---

[2] Accounts of Potter's character and his early days in Wisconsin, given in connection with the story of his famous duel, appeared frequently in local newspapers. The near-duel was a perennial "feature" story. Cf., for example, stories in the Chicago *Times,* Aug. 10, 1885; the Chicago *Tribune,* Dec. 24, 1882, Feb. 29, 1896; Milwaukee *Wisconsin,* April 28, May 10, 1891; Milwaukee *Sentinel,* March 15, 25, April 8, 1900, July 10, 1921; the Milwaukee *Journal,* Nov. 7, Dec. 6, 1920; the Burlington *Journal,* Jan. 27, 1926. Most of these accounts appear to have been based on one another, and some of them garbled badly the details of the affair. The Indian story was told by John G. Gregory of Milwaukee to Manuel Leno, a former student in the University of Wisconsin. Manuel Leno to the writer, July 26, 1942. Mr. Gregory, a retired journalist and historian, had long been interested in Potter's career and often wrote about Potter and the famous bowie knife incident.

[3] William F. Raney, *Wisconsin: A Story of Progress* (New York, 1940), 183; Milwaukee *Wisconsin,* April 28, 1891.

[4] Madison *Argus and Democrat,* Sept. 13, 1858.

Potter served in Congress from 1857 to 1863. Almost immediately upon his arrival in Washington he began to display a new and hitherto unsuspected truculence. He developed aptitude for the hair-splitting niceties of parliamentary law and he brought a biting sarcasm into debates on the slavery issue.[5] Moreover, sa᠎ ᠎he᠎Democrats, he "ranted of his chivalry in a tone that would have shamed any aspirant to rank among the F.F's of Virginia."[6]

Hardly had the Wisconsin representative settled into his congressional seat when he was involved in a fist fight in the aisles and received a challenge to a duel. On this occasion, Congressman Barksdale of Mississippi was haranguing the House on the evils of abolitionism and the crimes of the abolitionists. Galusha Grow of Pennsylvania, temporarily presiding over the House, called the Mississippian to order. Then, as Grow passed down the aisle, two Southerners sprang upon him. Potter immediately leaped into the fray, and in the melee Congressman Barksdale lost his wig and the Wisconsin congressman received a black eye. Some days later a sarcastic editorial ridiculing Barksdale appeared in the Baltimore *Sun*. Blaming Potter, the Mississippian sent him a challenge to a duel. To Barksdale's surprise, Potter appeared willing to meet his challenger in a closed room in Washington. This was contrary to the *code duello,* and Barksdale's seconds attempted to effect a reconciliation. They induced Potter to deny that he had written the offending article and to say that he had no connection with the Baltimore paper. Barksdale was satisfied with this explanation and withdrew his challenge.[7]

Twice more before this Congress ended, Representative Potter was in the headlines as a belligerent figure. Once he

[5] Burlington *Journal*, Jan. 27, 1926.
[6] Madison *Argus and Democrat*, Oct. 15, 1858.
[7] Milwaukee *Wisconsin*, April 28, 1891.

arose in Congress to deny a newspaper report that he had been in a fight with a Tennessee member, and once he was brought, after some resistance, to the bar of the House and fined for deliberate absenteeism.[8]

Back home in Wisconsin the Republicans rejoiced. Although the Democrats scorned his record, pointing out that he had done nothing but talk and win himself a black eye, the Republicans renominated Potter for Congress. The Democrats, professing to be thoroughly outraged, even sank to discrediting the congressman's courage. Barksdale, they asserted, was an old man, but old as he was, Potter would not have dared to attack him had not Congressman C. C. Washburn been there to help him.[9] But this scurrilous attempt to impugn their representative's bravery was promptly rebuked by the voters. They sent John F. Potter back to Congress.

Throughout most of the first session of the thirty-sixth Congress, Representative Potter peacefully performed his duties as an inconspicuous member of the Committee on Public Lands and as chairman of the Committee on Revolutionary Pensions. Such routine activities gave little opportunity for the exercise of his peculiar legislative talents. But, as Potter remained quiet, the sectional controversy waxed in intensity. Members of Congress quarreled with one another and vied in making bellicose speeches for the record. As spring came, and the dates for the nominating conventions drew near, nervousness and irritability increased.

On April 5, in an atmosphere surcharged with emotion, Owen Lovejoy made a violent speech against slavery and the Democratic Party. The Illinois congressman was the brother

---

[8] Madison *Argus and Democrat,* March 6, Oct. 1, 1858.
[9] *Ibid.,* Oct. 21, 1858.

of the Rev. Elijah Lovejoy, who was the only authentic martyr in the abolitionist crusade. Ever since his brother's death at the hands of an Alton mob, Owen Lovejoy had cried for revenge upon slavery and the South. On this April afternoon he had reached the climax of his denunciad and was gesticulating wildly as he stood in front of the Democratic side of the house.

Immediately Roger Pryor was on his feet. It was bad enough for delicate Southern ears to have to listen to Lovejoy's tirades, but the gentleman from Illinois could not come across to their side of the hall and shake his fist in their faces. Other Democrats sprang up, supporting Pryor. Republican members rushed to Lovejoy's side—among them Wisconsin's John F. Potter, his great black mustache bristling. Insults were hurled. "Negro thief!" cried one Southern gentleman to Lovejoy, while Mississippi's Barksdale called out: "The meanest Negro in the South is your superior." Reporters hurried about to catch the utterances of the nation's statesmen; the speaker pounded for order, and the sergeant-at-arms quieted the members before they gave more than verbal expression to their opinions. Lovejoy, the climax of his oration lost by the interruption, concluded his remarks from the front of the House.[10]

When, a few days after this affray, the official record of the debates appeared, Pryor discovered that Potter had shouted, "This side shall be heard, let the consequences be what they may." Up arose Pryor to assert that Potter had inserted these bold words in the record, but that he had not uttered them. Potter, equally indignant, admitted that he had inserted the words later, but declared he had uttered them at the time. Moreover, the Wisconsin congressman announced he would stand by what he had said.

---

[10] New York *Times,* April 6, 10, 1860; New York *Tribune,* April 13, 1860.

This was more than the sensitive Southern honor could bear. Enlisting the services of a second, Pryor immediately sent a note asking Potter to name a place, outside the District of Columbia, where he would receive further communications. Observing the punctilio of the *code duello,* Potter withdrew from the House, bade farewell to his wife, and drove to the rooms of Congressman C. C. Washburn. Quickly there assembled in those rooms Pennsylvania's Galusha Grow and Maine's Israel Washburn of the House of Representatives and Senators Zach Chandler and Ben Wade. There they agreed upon strategy, selected Colonel F. W. Landers to act as Potter's second, and sent him to say that Potter would not leave the District, but would accept a challenge in it. Immediately, Pryor's second delivered a note from his principal demanding "the satisfaction usual among gentlemen." Potter was glad to oblige, and offered to meet the offended Virginian in a closed room with bowie knives of equal size and weight and length of blade within twelve hours.

Upon sending his second with the challenge, Congressman Pryor had promptly withdrawn from the District of Columbia and was seven miles away in Alexandria, Virginia. He did not see Potter's acceptance, for his second, after consulting the challenger's outraged friends, replied that the terms suggested were vulgar, barbarous and inhuman, and asked for other weapons. Colonel Landers refused to consider any alteration, and since he thought the terms of the refusal reflected upon him, offered to meet Pryor or his second at any place. But this bravado was merely formal. The Virginian replied, through his second, that he had no quarrel with Colonel Landers and had meant no offense.

After this interchange, the police of the District stepped in, placed both Potter and Pryor under arrest, and released them under bonds of $5,000 to preserve the peace. Both congressmen returned to their seats to receive congratulations from their friends.[11]

While the principals in this ludicrous incident were exchanging notes and insults, the newspapers were squeezing the last drop of partisan sensationalism from it. Washington correspondents scurried about the capital city gathering rumors to send their papers. At home, Republican editors wrote solemn editorials praising Potter's willingness to defy Southern braggadocio, or deploring his risking his life at the demand of a Southern bully. Pryor was making, said the editors, "a cheap display of valor"; it was a "paltry performance."[12] In serious vein they discussed whether, under the code, there were real grounds for a duel.[13] Then, when the outcome was known, they all agreed that Potter had made Pryor ridiculous, and with one accord they agreed to laugh at the discomfiture of the Southern chivalry.[14] From all parts of the country bowie knives came to Congressman Potter, and the Missouri delegation to the Chicago Convention carried a seven-foot bowie knife to present to the redoubtable champion of Northern honor.[15]

Democratic comment was somewhat more realistic than the Republican. The first reaction of the Democrats of Wisconsin was to point out that state law forbade dueling, and to demand Potter's resignation.[16] On second thought, they concluded that "the whole affair is disgusting, and in our opinion reflects no credit on either side—Potter behaved indecently imprudent, and Pryor acted like a braggart fool."[17] Moreover, they recalled that the time for congres-

---

11 *Ibid.*, April 13–17, 1860; New York *Times,* April 13–21, 1860.
12 *Ibid.*, April 12, 13, 1860.
13 New York *Tribune,* April 14, 1860.
14 *Ibid.*, April 15, 17, 1860.
15 Madison *Argus and Democrat,* May 19, 28, 1860.
16 *Wisconsin Daily Patriot,* April 18, 1860.
17 *Ibid.*, April 19, 1860.

sional nominations was near, and they suspected that Potter was trying by "some exhibition of foolhardy and ruffianly valor" to "get into the papers."[18]

When Milwaukee and Racine Republicans prepared a reception for the valorous congressman, the Democrats were sure that politics lay at the bottom of his bravery.[19] "He is a candidate for reëlection," said the Chicago *Times,* and "if he should find it necessary to make another horrible threat to excite still further the enthusiasm of his Republican friends, we may rest assured that horrible threat will be made."[20]

The Democratic analysis of the bowie knife duel was supported by Carl Schurz. "People threw up their hats when the news came . . ." he wrote Potter. "Republicans congratulated each other and Democrats swore they would vote for you the next time. The question whether you will be renominated and reëlected seems to be settled. All those that had any aspirations that way will have to hang up their harps. . . . You will see the effect of your course next fall."[21]

In the fall Potter was reëlected, and he served another term in Congress. For the remainder of his life, he was "Bowie Knife" Potter, and the story of his affair with Pryor grew large in the fertile soil of his admirers' imaginations. Years later, in an interview, he remembered details of the incident which were not known at the time. But he saw it, as well, from a different perspective. "I thought," he recalled "that he would not fight, and that would have a good result by throwing derision upon dueling and the Southern bravos." He remembered, too, "We all felt that the time had

---

[18] Madison *Argus and Democrat,* April 20, 1860.
[19] *Ibid.,* April 24, May 5, 1860.
[20] *Wisconsin Daily Patriot,* April 24, May 7, 1860.
[21] Schurz to Potter, April 17, 1860, Milwaukee *Sentinel,* March 25, 1900.

come for some Northern man to lay aside his scruples and strike one blow that would convince the South that we were not to be bullied any longer."[22]

Here, in Potter's memory, lay the whole change which had come over the United States. The willingness to challenge and to accept challenges had supplanted the old spirit of compromise. A week after Pryor and Potter returned to the House, the Democrats assembled in Charleston. To the gathering came Northerners intent upon forcing Stephen A. Douglas upon the party and determined not to be bullied any longer. Their spirit was the same that John F. Potter had displayed—and they met the sentiments of Roger Pryor. They split the Democratic Party and thereby elected Abraham Lincoln President. Even then, conservative men, remembering the old American way, sought to save the Union through concession and conciliation. They failed—not because the machinery of the nation was broken, but because the spirit of compromise was gone.

---

[22] W. A. Croffut, "John F. Potter and His Bowie Knife Incident," Chicago *Tribune,* Dec. 24, 1882.

SEVEN

Regions, Classes, and Sections in American History

HISTORIANS have long been aware of the significance of sections in the development of the United States. Since Frederick Jackson Turner first propounded his frontier hypothesis, students have given increasing attention to the influence of the West, the North, and the South in America's evolution. From the exhaustive monographs of historians it is apparent that sectionalism has ever been a divisive force in the nation. Only a long series of compromises has held the nation together. The divergent interests of sections have constituted the major problem of America's past and bid fair to be the major issues of the future.

Recognizing the conflicts between sections, recent students—designating themselves "regionalists"—have attempted to break down the accepted historical sections into regions and to create a "new science of the region." This new science is, in the words of two of its protagonists, "descriptive of how all societies grow, fundamental to realistic planning, and important in the interrelation and coördina-

Reprinted by permission from the *Journal of Land & Public Utility Economics,* 20: 35–44 (February, 1944).

tion of the social sciences." Students of regionalism attempt to interpret the living society of the historical nation and the quest for political, cultural, and spiritual autonomy. In the end, the regionalists hope to bring the work of ecologists, geographers, sociologists, and economists to focus on the region and to produce a program for regional development within a unified nation. Hopefully they assert that these studies would lay the groundwork for national planning which would preserve the beneficial qualities of each region and utilize the full economic and cultural potentialities of each for the well-being of the whole. In contrast with the divisive, selfish nature of sectionalism, this "regional-nationalism" would promote unity and coöperation.

Whatever may be the outcome of such studies, it must be apparent at once that no research into the nature and function of the region can be valid which is not based upon a thorough knowledge of the role which regions have played in American history. On the other hand, historians—long accustomed to envisaging the nation in terms of sectional conflict—might well consider whether regionalism offers a satisfactory concept upon which to base a synthesis of the complex forces in American development.

The regionalists' basic concept that the United States is a congeries of regions is fundamentally sound. Geographically, its territory consists of an almost infinite variety of regions ranging from the coastal plains of the Atlantic seaboard to the arid deserts of the Southwest. Considered in their cultural aspects, an even greater variety of regions may be defined. There are metropolitan regions and their hinterlands, regions of sparse population, regions of specialized farming, regions of literary activity, and regions of artistic striving. There are mill zones, trade areas, milk sheds, federal reserve districts, army corps areas, freight rate territories, and cotton kingdoms. Regionalism is a concept predicated upon the assumption that American life is organized on local bases. Regions of economic production, of public health, of police administration, and of national defense necessarily overlap but are not necessarily coterminous. Regions may be marked differently for different purposes and at different times; yet, regardless of the frame of reference, the persistence of the region becomes the one constant factor in the American scene.

The first and most stable of all regional classifications— and the one most significant in American history—is based upon physiography. The settlement of the continent proceeded from the seacoast to the Ohio and Mississippi valleys, over the Great Plains and the Rockies to the Pacific. Within each of these areas there were regions whose essential character was determined by the climate, rainfall, topography, vegetation, and natural transportation facilities. In the colonial period, settlement followed the configuration of the country and no less than eight regions were apparent by the time of the American Revolution. These were the New England seacoast, the New England river valleys, the valley of the Hudson, the Delaware and Schuylkill valleys, the Chesapeake tidewater, the Carolina rice coast, the Virginia and Carolina piedmont, and the Appalachian highlands. During and immediately after the Revolution, migrating colonists began the settlement of the Ohio Valley, the Kentucky Bluegrass and the Cumberland Plateau. Soon Whitney's invention created the cotton kingdom. Sugar cane took root in Louisiana and population moving westward occupied the upper shore of the Mississippi, followed the winding course of the Missouri, and struck out over the plains and mountains for the Oregon country.

Each region met by the advancing peoples possessed a distinctive geographic character and in each region the settlers took on characteristics identified by their environment. In the process of settlement regions changed their character, their people, and even their boundaries. The industrial revolution transformed the river valleys of New England into mill zones, laid iron trails across the prairies, dug tortuous caverns beneath the Appalachian hills, and piled up mountainous heaps of barren slag. Tidewater regions lost their soil and grew up in second-growth slash while irrigation ditches made deserts blossom. Yet regions remained. The nation was born in the region, and the region remained as the dominant force in the nation.

Beginning with this concept of the American nation as a series of regions, students of both regionalism and history should recognize that the population of the nation is divided within itself into sundry economic, cultural and social groups. From the beginning of settlement on the western continent there has been a constant evolution of groups and a constant conflict between social classes. In the first days of the white man in the Chesapeake tidewater, social and class differences developed. Before the first representative assembly met in Virginia—with the first division of land by the London Company—American class distinctions began. Those planters who, by virtue of greater wealth, superior ability, or political favoritism, secured the better lands of the Virginia river bottoms constituted a favored class in the colony. Later arrivals and less-favored settlers found themselves forced into the back country or out to the frontier. The river bottom planters, with their own wharves, used their commanding position to exploit their less fortunate neighbors. The shipment of colonial tobacco was in the hands of the nascent planter aristocracy. Controlling the colony's courts as it did, this aristocracy administered a planter's justice. Through its domination of the colonial assembly, it limited the political privileges of the newer settlements which the less-favored groups established.

In each of the colonial regions a comparable situation developed. The Quakers of Philadelphia, the landlords of Maryland, the merchants of New York, and the merchant-shipbuilders of the New England seacoast became the dominant groups in their regions, and other groups were faced with the choice of yielding to them or migrating to another region. Yet, within each new settlement, the process of group division was repeated. One group seized and held the wealth-producing vantage points and dominated the region. In the valley of Virginia those Scotch-Irish who gained the bottom lands forced their fellows into the less fertile hills. Having done so, the local rulers made an alliance with the planters of the tidewater, secured special privileges and won control of their local parish vestries and of the county courts. "Come-outers" of New England migrated to the river valleys and divided like cells again and again, each time leaving a predominant and one or more subordinate groups to continue the struggle for control of the region. In the settlement of the frontier there were always class distinctions. Those who acquired the best lands constituted a dominant group. Those with the poorer soils or those removed from immediate access to the lines of transportation became economic, political, and cultural subordinates.

The contest between groups for the control of their region has been the moving force in American history. The control of a region involves the possession and manipulation of all those social, political, and economic institutions which affect its people. First among these institutions are the local agencies of government and of politics. Because of the regional nature of the nation, American government and politics have always been based upon local interests. The largest portion of the tax dollar has, until recently, been expended for local government—for police protection, streets and highways, poor relief, and education. Except in emergency situations, local government (its policies and practices) makes the greatest impact on the individual. National politics are frequently a composite of local policies, and Winfield Scott Handcock's oft-ridiculed remark that "the tariff is a local issue" showed an insight into the realities of that much-debated "national" problem.

Because of the primary importance of local government, the economic or social group which can control wards, townships, and counties can direct the expenditure of local taxes, determine the location of streets and highways, direct the operations of police officers, create zones, and formulate the ordinances, rulings, decisions, and laws which mark the bounds of local conduct. Through control of local governments, Southern planters could once prevent slaves from escaping from bondage and can still hold sharecroppers in peonage. Through the control of local governments, manufacturers can prevent strikers from molesting strikebreakers, landlords can evade building inspectors, and iron foundries can ignore smoke-abatement ordinances. Hence, planters, manufacturers, landlords, and iron magnates—each a group dominant in its region—contribute to the war chests of the local parties and coöperate with ward heelers or civic organizations in "getting out the vote." "American" politics are regional politics, and the control of local and state governments is the prime consideration of ruling groups.

In a democracy, however, the control of political institutions cannot be obtained without the assistance of the intellectual institutions of the region. Unless schools, press, and pulpit further the ideological concepts of the rulers in classrooms, sermons, and editorials, and unless libraries, forums, theaters, lectures, and lyceums render assistance by suppressing opposing views and advancing "constructive" opinion, the dominant group in any region will lose its supremacy and become subordinate to whatever other group may obtain control over the complex agencies of mass education.

Because they serve the interests of local groups, schools have always been locally financed and controlled. Public schools are supported by local taxes, and their teachers are hired by local boards. No widespread enthusiasm has ever been aroused for a national university, and the pressure of a thousand local communities has forestalled a department of education in the Federal government. Of more than a thousand colleges in the United States, only a handful can claim more than local support, while the great "national" universities are primarily concerned with serving special regions. The majority of the faculties of the great universities are natives of the immediate region, the majority of the students live within a hundred and fifty miles of the campus, and the majority of the alumni live within driving distance. The graduate students study local social conditions, local soil, or local economics, and upon receiving their degrees get teaching positions in nearby colleges.

The essential localism of the schools render them particularly subservient to the dominant groups of the region. The curriculum tends to reflect the prevailing group concepts and is designed to further group control. The first American public school law—"The Old Deluder Satan Law" of colonial Massachusetts—declared that schools were weapons in the fight against the devil. The curriculum of the New England schools emphasized the necessity of obedience to the Puritans' economic and religious ideals. In a later generation Horace Mann "sold" public education to the rising manufacturers of New England with the assertion that education would support manufacturing, increase invention, and produce a docile laboring population. More recently, the Morrill Act furnished the dominant groups in agricultural regions with special schools, and the development of trade courses and vocational high schools has served the interests of dominant urban industrial or labor groups.

Like the school, the church reflects the opinions of local dominant groups. Unlike the school, the church makes claims to national influence, but the regional character of the churches belie the claims. Congregationalists, Baptists, and Presbyterians are frankly organized on a regional or local basis. The Methodist annual conferences and the Episcopal dioceses are practically autonomous units. Theology varies with regions, and there is a greater difference between the constituent churches of a denomination than between the denominations in a given region. Southern Baptists differ less from Southern Methodists than they do from Northern Baptists. Each church yields to the pressures of its region and becomes a supporter of its dominant group. Anglican clergymen in colonial Virginia furnished spiritual justification to Virginia's planters, and the Congregational ministers of New England preached the Revolutionary War as a holy crusade. Along the frontier and in the back country, Presbyterian pulpiteers indoctrinated their Scotch-Irish parishioners with the precepts of a divinely-ordained squatter sovereignty. In the beginning, Methodists and Presbyterians in the South opposed slavery. Before the sectional controversy had been settled by civil war, the Southern Methodists and Presbyterians had churches of their own and were devoting their efforts to proving that slavery was a divine institution.

Control of a region's political and intellectual institutions is merely ancillary to the control of the purely economic institutions which lie at the foundation of a region's life. The ownership of the banks and the direction of credit facilities; the control of railroads, harbors, shipping facilities, and warehouses; and the dominance of employers' associations, chambers of commerce, and labor organizations are the major objectives of a region's ruling group.

American history has known few regions in which one group has secured absolute dominance and held power for an appreciable period. Instead, the contending groups have customarily been nearly balanced, the superior group maintaining only a precarious hold on power. Occasionally this power has been held by coercion; more generally it has been held by sundry concessions to subordinate groups, and sometimes it has been held by a skillful process of dividing the opposition.

The dynamic force in American history has been the struggle of rival groups for the control of their regions. The evolution of an area from a hunters' and trappers' paradise into a metropolitan region, through all the stages of lumbering, farming, and village life, is dependent upon the struggle of successive dominant groups for control. Thus, the lumberman challenged the control of the trapper; the farmer pushed out to claim the land as the lumberman, his timber gone, relinquished his hold; then the farmer in turn became subordinate to the rising business interests of the village. Within the village a mercantile group fell under the control of the bankers, who became the nucleus for a group of industrialists. At every step in this competition, the dominant group has sought to maintain its control by using the power of the government, by determining the policies of press, church and school, and by encouraging or resisting the growth of economic institutions.

The primary motivation for this competition between social and economic groups has been the extraction of profit and prestige from the region's resources. The control of the region is the first and greatest need of the dominant group.

But this control can be secured only by keeping a careful watch on outside influences. Under the American system, regions constitute component parts of a diverse nation. The development of any one of them may be halted, modified, or hastened by the action of extra-regional power. The federal or the state governments may adopt policies which promote or deter the advance of groups within the region. Freight rates, interest rates, or the incidence of taxation may favor the advance of one group over another. Hence the controlling group within each region has sought to combine with groups in other regions to control these outside forces and to divert their actions from evil to good.

Such a combination of interregional groups has been possible only upon a basis of mutual concession and agreement. Complete identity of interests between groups of different regions has seldom been evident, but their harmonious coöperation has generally been possible through compromise. When the dominant group of one region has succeeded in making a working alliance with comparable groups elsewhere, the result has been a political party, and the terms of the compromise have been formulated in a party platform or in a party's legislative program.

Frequently, of course, the dominant group of one region has been the enemy of the ruling class in another. Often, the sole unifying factor in a political combination has been a common enemy. The dominant group in east Tennessee from 1830 to 1860, for example, was Whig; yet east Tennessee's small-farming, non-slaveholding Whigs had little in common with the great Whig planters of the Black Belts. The Whigs of east and west Tennessee were cultural, social and economic opposites; yet their common enmity to the Democrats brought them together in state and national politics. So, too, the Whig planters of the Cotton Kingdom had few interests in common with the American-System men of the north. They opposed the bank, tariff, and internal improvement program of Clay, Adams and Webster—yet a common enmity to Jacksonianism drew them into the Whig ranks. Primarily, the Southern Whigs were interested in maintaining their social and economic dominance in the Southern regions; mutual conservatism brought them into political alliance with Northern bankers, contractors and industrialists. Since Reconstruction, the conservative, frugal Bourbons of the South have been allied with the often-extravagant, frequently-corrupt, and occasionally-radical groups of Northern and Eastern cities. Not community of interests but a common enmity and a common desire to dominate their own regions have put these strange bed-fellows into a single political berth.

From the beginning, just as group competition for regional control has constituted the dynamic force in American history, so the system of compromise between regional groups has been the cohesive factor in American life. A common opposition to the English parliamentary program brought Southern planters, New England merchants, back-country farmers, and Scotch-Irish frontiersmen together in the American Revolution. The Declaration of Independence, with its egalitarian philosophy, had little appeal to the wealthier classes in colonial communities, but only through a momentary adherence to that radical document could the economic shackles be avoided. Upon the conclusion of the war, an internal conflict ensued within the various regions of the new United States. Merchant groups in New England, planters in the South, and businessmen in the Middle States struggled with radical groups for the control of the political and economic machinery of the regions. In town meetings, in counties, and in states the conflict went on throughout a lustrum which was indeed a "critical period" for all the groups concerned. In the end, conservative groups gained control of a number of state governments. Immediately they began to legislate in their own interests, and immediately the radical groups began rebelling against the legislation of the victors.

It was with a full realization that only a strong national government could insure their gains in their regions that the dominant conservative groups assembled at Philadelphia. They met to form that "more perfect union" which would promote "domestic tranquility." The interests of merchants and planters were antipathetic. The tobacco growers of Virginia and Maryland had little in common with the producers of rice and indigo in South Carolina. Land speculators and shippers were at opposite poles on matters of national policy. Yet they had one common interest—the desire to secure and maintain dominance in their respective regions.

The resultant Constitution was the platform of the political party which these groups founded. In the drafting of that platform there were conflicts which had to be settled by compromises, and in the completed document there were ambiguous passages which represented verbally the decision to postpone the issue until after the Constitution should have run the gauntlet of the ratifying conventions. But the greatest of the compromises of the Constitution was the document itself. It was a compromise between what the members of the Philadelphia convention wanted and what they believed their opponents desired.

With the adoption of the Constitution and the establishment of the Federal government there began a struggle for the control of the agencies of national power. The struggle was between regional groups. Hamilton's program, unfolded in the first years of the new government, was a frank attempt to align the dominant groups of certain regions behind the national government and to use the power of the government to benefit the supporting groups. Unfortunately for his purposes, Hamilton's program could not encompass the planters' groups which dominated the Southern regions. These groups made the minimum number of compromises necessary to keep peace in their respective regions and began to combine with subordinate groups—whiskey rebels along the frontier, ex-Shaysites of New England, small farmers of the Middle States, and artisans of Eastern urban communities—to seize the national government from Hamilton's Federalists. Each of the groups entering into this new combination was primarily interested in securing the dominance of its own region. The Jeffersonian concepts of strict construction and of states' rights served merely as a device for holding the groups together. It was another political platform comparable to the Declaration of Independence and the Constitution. Once the Jeffersonian groups gained power, the principles of the Kentucky and Virginia Resolutions were ignored by their authors and were adopted by the ousted Federalists. But no sooner had the Jeffersonian groups gained power than they began to separate. United momentarily by offense against a common enemy, they found their interests opposed when they came to exercise the power they had won. Immediately the groups began to form new alignments, and shortly there appeared a new political party with its own formula. Time and again this process has been repeated in American political history: never has a party succeeded in gaining and holding the support of all the dominant groups of all the regions.

Fundamentally, the reason for this constant flux of political alignments is to be found in the imperialism of the dominant groups. No group has ever been content with the simple control of its own region. Instead, each group—upon achieving control of its region—has sought to extend its imperium and make tributaries of adjacent regions. Once a group is securely ensconced in its own area, it attempts to secure the political machinery of neighboring regions, to impose its ideological concepts on its neighbors, and to direct the economic activities of those regions for its own ends. Thus a metropolitan area under the control of industrialists seeks to control its state's government, to influence the teaching in the state's schools, and to utilize the power of the state to make the rural hinterlands tributary to the metropolis. Such a metropolitan region under the control of a labor group seeks the same ends and employs comparable tactics. In the same way the rural areas, controlling the government of a state, promote agricultural education, impose discriminatory taxes upon urban wealth, and direct the expenditure of state funds (extracted from the metropolis) to build farm-to-market roads, carry on soil conservation projects, or give Bangs tests to cattle.

It is the imperialism of dominant groups that has given rise to the phenomenon of sectionalism in American history. Sectionalism is the combination of comparable dominant groups in contiguous regions in order to exploit other regions or the nation as a whole. Through the control of state governments and political parties, such a combination of groups can coerce the national government. Repeatedly in American history sectional combinations have been able to dictate the choice of a President, block unfavorable legislation, secure favorable laws, and extract an undue proportion of federal appropriations for sectional benefit. Sectionalism is competitive rather than coöperative; it is directed toward particularistic rather than national ends. It is divisive rather than unifying in its tendencies, and its implications are conservative rather than progressive.

Sectionalism began in American history with the program of Alexander Hamilton. Although the first secretary of the treasury designed his financial arrangements to appeal to the creditor groups in all regions, he gained adherents primarily in New York and New England. The Jeffersonian opposition was national rather than sectional; but by 1812 the opponents of the Republicans had created a new sectionalism in the old Federalist centers. Thereafter, sectional alignments were a constant threat to the Union. The Southern section, composed of the Cotton Kingdom and the adjacent principalities of rice, tobacco, and sugar, constituted a single political bloc from 1820 to 1860. Efforts to unite Northern regions in an opposing section began with Henry Clay's American System and continued until a sectional party had placed Abraham Lincoln in the White House.

Such sectional alignments of minority groups usually found themselves in a strong bargaining position and were generally able to force compromises and concessions from other regional groups. The great compromises of 1820, 1833, and 1850—each forced by sectional interests—were only the dramatic and publicized symbols of hundreds of other less spectacular but no less important compromises. Political platforms, party programs, and congressional legislation were filled with compromises between the sections. The eventual refusal of one section to yield to another led to secession and the Civil War.

The years after the Civil War witnessed the first complete victory of a sectional party. During the Reconstruction period, the captains of industry and the masters of the counting houses dominated the Northern and Eastern regions. The basic conflict between these leaders of society and laborers and farmers was momentarily stilled because the masters of capital had control both of the state and national governments and of the Republican party. They controlled the intellectual life of the country through endowments to private schools, election of the officers of public schools, and the imposition of "patriotic" concepts upon academic cur-

ricula. Press and church became "big business" and devoted
their efforts to propagating the ideals of the sectionally
dominant groups. Moreover, these groups in the Northern
and Eastern regions had the alliance of Western regions. In
the West, industrial groups were coming into power and
Western finance was intimately connected with Eastern
financial centers. Moreover, in the legislation of the period,
Western regions received railroads, internal improvements,
free lands, and improved credit facilities. Whatever opposition might have developed locally in the West was stayed by
Eastern control of the agencies of public expression. The
Eastern groups controlled Western newspapers through
bank loans, stock ownership and the control of news services.
The Western church was subservient to its Eastern leaders,
and both the Democratic and the Republican parties were
controlled by Easterners. For the most part, any minor
rumblings of discontent could be silenced by the oratorical
waving of the bloody shirt from political stumps.

Together, these Eastern and Western groups prepared to
exploit the South. To make sure that they controlled the
national government, they gave the suffrage to Southern
Negroes. The dominance remained secure until the Negroes
gained sufficient political experience to demand concessions
for themselves. Finally, confronted with the imminent possibility that a new alignment between Western farmers,
Southern poor whites, and Negroes would overthrow them,
the masters of capital of the Eastern regions discarded the
Negroes and entered into a new combination with the
Southern Bourbons. The sectional dominance of the Northern regions had lasted long enough, however, to give the
masters of capital a firm grasp upon the economic institutions of the conquered South.

Fully aware of the divisive and exploitative aspects of
sectionalism, modern regionalists have proposed the sub-

stitution of a nationalism based upon regional integration in the total national picture. But any "planning" for such a goal should be firmly grounded upon a recognition of the historical nature of American regions. The study of regional history might serve to clarify the issues for both historians and regionalists. Historians would do well to recognize that the United States is a congeries of regions for whose possession rival groups have been engaged in a continuous struggle. The nature and evolution of the regions have been determined by this conflict, and national history is the product of the complex struggle for regional control and group expansion. Such a regional approach to American history offers no simple formula for resolving the complexities of American development, but it presents a more realistic basis for evaluating past and present American problems.

Regionalists who envisage a systematic plan for national well-being with the goal of the "greatest good for the greatest number" not only must consider geographic and mechanistic regions but also must concern themselves with the constant struggle between rival and competitive groups in the regions. National planning which ignores the facts of group dominance or fails to analyze the techniques of group control is doomed to failure. Any program of national planning must be based upon a realistic recognition of group conflict and must incorporate a program of conciliation in which Southern sharecroppers and New York bankers, the railroad managements and the railroad brotherhoods, the C.I.O. and the A.F. of L., the potato growers of Maine and Idaho and the hotel proprietors of California and Florida can lie down together as lambs. Unless the regionalist program can comprehend all groups in all regions and can organize all factions in support of a united and prosperous nation it will degenerate, in the end, into a new sectionalism.

EIGHT

Abraham Lincoln and
the Politicians

THE people, declared the twenty-eight-year-old legisla-
tor, were not suffering great injuries. "No Sir, it is the
politician who is the first to sound the alarm. . . . It is he,
who, by these unholy means, is endeavoring to blow up a
storm that he may ride upon and direct. . . . This movement is exclusively the work of politicians; a set of men
who have interests aside from the interests of the people,
and who, to say the most of them, are, taken as a mass, at
least one long step removed from honest men."[1]

For the remaining half of his life, Abraham Lincoln
clung to his opinion of politicians. Although he added the
ruefully facetious remark, "I say this with the greater freedom because, being a politician myself, none can regard it
as personal," he mainly reserved the term for his opponents,
and especially for Democrats. "If the politicians and leaders

---

Read before the third annual Civil War Conference sponsored
by Gettysburg College, November 19–21, 1959. Reprinted by permission from *Civil War History*, 6: 43–55 (March, 1960).

[1] Roy P. Basler, ed., *Collected Works of Abraham Lincoln* (New
Brunswick, 1953), I, 65–66.

of parties were as true as the people, there would be little fear," he told a crowd in Lawrenceburg, Indiana, on his fifty-second birthday. Three days later, in Pittsburgh, he explained in words reminiscent of his speech in the Illinois legislature: ". . . *there is no crisis,* except such a one as may be gotten up at any time by designing politicians."[2] "You are quite a female politician," he told Jesse Frémont when she irritated him by explaining the effect her husband's emancipation order would have on British sentiment.[3] "May I inquire how long it took you and the New York politicians to concoct that paper?" he asked a group of Tennesseans who protested against Andrew Johnson's arrangements for the election of 1864.[4]

Yet, however low his opinion of politicians, Abraham Lincoln took an active interest in the minutiae of politics. Formally he could advise a Young Man's Lyceum to let "reverence for the laws . . . become the political religion of the nation," while from the elevated post of congressman he could instruct young Billy Herndon on forming a "Rough and Ready Club." "Take in everybody you can get . . . gather up all the shrewd wild boys about town. . . . Let everyone play the part he can play best—some speak, some sing, and all hollow."[5] He added example to precept. He attended meetings, and, with more talent for speaking than for singing, he spoke on every occasion. He carefully surveyed the prospects of the Whigs in each electoral campaign, and once stood for election to the legislature only to resign upon winning. "I only allowed myself to be elected,"

2 *Ibid.,* IV, 197, 211.
3 Allen Nevins, *The War for the Union* (New York, 1959), I, 338, 428.
4 *Appleton's Annual Cyclopedia* (New York, 1888–1903), IV, 764–767.
5 Basler, *Collected Works of Abraham Lincoln,* I, 112.

he explained, "because it was thought my doing so would help [Richard] Yates."[6] He understood the necessity for preparing careful lists of voters and organizing them—and even for "working so quiet that the adversary shall not be notified." As for money, its use, "in the main," was wrong —"but for certain objects, in a political contest, the use of some, is both right and indispensable." So saying, he promised one hundred dollars to a prospective delegate to the Chicago Wigwam.[7] With so intimate a knowledge of the precepts and practice of politics, Lincoln found it easy, as President-elect, to deal with such experienced political engineers as Thurlow Weed and Simon Cameron.

He was fully, even keenly, aware of the role of patronage in building and maintaining a political party. When rumor reached Illinois in 1849 that Zachary Taylor was about to appoint Justin Butterfield as Commissioner of the General Land Office, Lincoln raised a hue and cry and wrote vigorously to leading Whigs to bring pressure on the President. Butterfield's appointment, he assured them, would be an "egregious political blunder." It would "dissatisfy, rather than gratify," the Whigs of Illinois. Butterfield was a "drone" who had "never spent a dollar or lifted a finger in the fight." "Shall this thing be?" he cried in anguish. "Our Whigs will throw down their arms and fight no more."[8]

Although he opposed Butterfield, Lincoln deplored factional rivalries for patronage crumbs. Struggles for political succession weakened parties. He made a virtue of his own inability to succeed himself in Congress, and used it to emphasize his "live and let live" policy. He refused to compete for the General Land Office post he would have liked, and tried to patch up a quarrel between two rival candidates

---

[6] *Ibid.*, II, 298.
[7] *Ibid.*, 412–413.
[8] *Ibid.*, 48–51.

for the place.[9] Withal, he was convinced, he told the secretary of the treasury, that national patronage should be dispensed through the advice of congressmen, and that President Taylor should not shirk his duty of leadership. "He must occasionally say, or seem to say, 'by the Eternal, I take the responsibility.' " Those were the lessons Jackson had taught—"and we dare not disregard the lessons of experience."[10]

With such ideas, and with the lessons of Jackson and Taylor both confirming them, Lincoln tackled the problems of the patronage in his own administration. It was, he quickly discovered, an unending task and he moaned frequently, even sometimes with humor, at the importunities of the office seekers. When he got the varioloid smallpox he wryly remarked that now he had something he could give everyone. No sooner was he nominated than well-wishers began to advise him to avoid factionalism in the party. William Cullen Bryant warned him against politicians interested only in their own advancement and, in words reminiscent of those that Nicholas Biddle gave to William Henry Harrison, proposed that Lincoln should give no pledges, make no speeches, write no letters. Lincoln assured him that he knew the danger and meant to avoid it. "Fairness to all" became his motto, and during the campaign he added as instruction to his workers "but commit me to nothing." In August 1860, he could assure Cassius M. Clay, who was so generally excluded from inner circles that he had come to suspect all gatherings as conspiracies, that "the cliques have not yet commenced upon me."[11]

After November he could no longer make such a statement. The cliques came down upon him; office seekers and

---

[9] See *ibid.*, I, 364–365, 431, 463; II, 41, 79.
[10] *Ibid.*, II, 32, 60.
[11] *Ibid.*, IV, 81, 83, 92, 114.

their supporters swarmed upon Springfield, followed him to Washington, and settled in his waiting room for the four years that he was in the White House. "Fairness to all" continued to be his watchword, and factionalism continued to distress him. "There is not a more foolish way of conducting a political rivalry," he sighed in 1864 when Kansas' Senator James H. Lane and Governor Thomas Carney were squabbling, "than these fierce and bitter struggles over the patronage."[12] His early efforts to avoid the cliques won even the approval of the Democratic New York *World*. "He has convinced us that the warm interest in his success, felt by all good men, is not thrown away upon a hard, hackneyed, truckling politician."[13]

Not all Democrats were so generous. In fact, the general tendency of the Democratic press was to apply the touchstone of partisanship to each successive act of the President and to see him constantly bending before political pressures. Samuel Medary's *Crisis* in Columbus, Ohio, was widely influential among Democratic journals and often set the tone of the opposition press. To Medary, Lincoln was the "mere instrument of designing cabals around him . . . influenced to the worst of acts and the most diabolical feats of folly." He was a "mere child" led by William H. Seward and Salmon P. Chase. His first annual message had a "partisan tone," he was "neither honest, capable, nor loyal," and he was completely in the hands of "abolition vipers" led by Horace Greeley. The Union Leagues, "a more desperate and bloody set of scamps than their cousins the Know Nothings," controlled him: "They dictate terms to Mr. Lincoln as though he were a mere piece of wax. Perhaps he is." He was in all things a "miserable tool"—although

---

[12] *Ibid.,* VII, 338.
[13] New York *World,* February 12, 1861.

even Medary admitted that it would be a national calamity if Lincoln died and Hannibal Hamlin became President. In fact, the Ohio editor was so enamored with the idea that Lincoln was a vacillating tool that he thought "if the Democrats should get control of the next Congress, Mr. Lincoln will not be the worst man they might find in the Presidential Chair. With better surroundings, we believe Mr. Lincoln would improve vastly."[14]

It took the New York *World* a little while to adopt Medary's viewpoint. In January, 1862, it hailed Edwin M. Stanton's appointment as secretary of war as evidence that Lincoln was "the servant of no clique, the pliant tool of no party, the self-deceived victim of no blinding fanaticism." The "practiced politicians" of his cabinet had gained no undue ascendency over him. He was, in fact, a "cool, wise, large-minded statesman." But then came September, 1862, with its Emancipation Proclamation, and the *World* saw the light. Lincoln had "been coerced by the insanity of the radicals, by the denunciation of their presses, by the threats of their governors." The proclamation was "not the measure of a statesman, but of a politician" with his eye on the approaching elections in New York.[15] Thereafter, the *World* called steady attention to Lincoln's partisan acts. When he called for 300,000 men, it was a "satire of statesmanship." When he removed General George B. McClellan, he had "yielded once more to their [Radicals'] insensate demands." When a cabinet crisis arose, Lincoln lacked "the nerve" to deal with it—"he quailed before the enmity of the excluded faction." Moreover, Lincoln's handling of the army was political, his letter to a Niagara conference was a

---

[14] Columbus (Ohio) *Crisis,* April 18, May 2, July 11, November 12, 1861; May 4, 1862; January 27, March 2, 1864.
[15] New York *World,* January 14, September 24, September 25, 1862.

scheme to entrap Republicans who were deserting to John
C. Frémont. But the *World's* analysis differed in the end
from that of the *Crisis*. Instead of seeing with Medary that
Lincoln had surrendered to faction, the New York paper
saw him engaged in "dextrous trimming" between factions
—giving the offices to one and adopting the principles of
the other, and frustrating himself in the process. Lincoln
substituted cunning for statesmanship.[16]

In frequent instances, the Democratic spokesmen were
guessing shrewdly. Many of Lincoln's acts were politically
inspired, and sometimes he yielded to pressure. But the
opposition, bemused by the factional conflict between Moderate and Radical Republicans, failed to perceive that Lincoln was using the patronage to build the Republicans into
a national party with himself at its head. Lincoln kept control of the patronage, subjecting himself to the ordeal of
listening to office-seekers, and doling out the appointments.
Years before, he had declared that Taylor should take, or
seem to take, the responsibility. Admiringly the New York
World, before it joined the opposition, recounted that
"once he puts down his foot, he puts it down firmly." He
was a "self-poised and self-dependent statesman." Rare it
was that he felt himself defeated by the conflicting pressures.
Once he threw the problem of a Honolulu commissioner
into Seward's lap: "In self-defense," he explained, "I am
disposed to say 'Make a selection and send it to me!' " But
such occasions were few. And even when he did not personally take the responsibility, he set the policy. The policy
was national. He consulted congressmen on appointments
in their districts—even on commissions in the army. When
Tyler was president, Lincoln insisted that congressmen be

---

[16] *Ibid.,* November 11, December 23, 1862; March 14, March 18,
1865.

consulted. Now he consulted them. "So far as I understand,
it is unprecedented [to] send an officer into a State against
the wishes of the members of Congress and of the same
party." He referred office seekers to the departments. He
agreed with William P. Fessenden that treasury appointments should have the secretary's advice and consent.[17] But
these were national officers. Lincoln made no gesture towards the local politicians or the political leaders of the
states. The patronage was national, and he used it, not primarily to balance factions but to build a national party.

Lincoln's primary task as a politician was to create a
national Republican party and to mold it into a serviceable
tool for the national welfare. The party which nominated
him and put him into the White House was an unorganized
conglomeration of opposition groups. Some of them had
been Loco-Focos, Barnburners, and then Free Soilers in
previous political incarnations. Some were anti-Nebraska
Democrats, some were the battered and shattered remnants
of the old Whig party. There were in the undisciplined
ranks which marched under the Republican banner, Mid-
dlewestern farmers who wanted a homestead law, Pennsylvania ironmongers hungering for a protective tariff, newly
arrived immigrants and old Know Nothings who wanted
nothing to do with each other. The party stood, in common
with Breckinridge Democrats, for a Pacific railroad and for
states' rights. It was more certain on what it stood against:
It was opposed to Stephen A. Douglas, James Buchanan, the
Devil, and the Democrats.

Lincoln had played a minor part in preserving the con-
fusion. In 1848 he had thought it absurd to make a platform
for a national party. It was "the true philosophy of govern-

---

[17] Basler, *Collected Works of Abraham Lincoln,* IV, 302. See also
ibid., V, 147; VII, 423.

ment," he said, "that congress should represent all opinions and principles, and when the wisdom of all had been compared and united," the will of the people should prevail.[18] As the election of 1860 drew near, Lincoln advised caution on Republicans. They should not insert into state platforms items which, however popular they might be in a particular locality, would do harm to Republicans elsewhere. He pointed to the anti-foreign sentiment in Massachusetts, the enforcement of the Fugitive Slave Law in New Hampshire and its repeal in Ohio, and squatter sovereignty in Kansas. "In these things there is explosive enough to blow up half a dozen national conventions, if it gets into them." He was not "wedded" to the party platform system, and preferred to have men chosen to office on "their records and antecedents."[19] There was but one item upon which all Republicans were agreed—opposition to the extension of slavery to the territories—and Lincoln succeeded in keeping it to the fore. Yet when he was elected—on a platform which was like a pair of suspenders long enough for any man and short enough for any boy—Lincoln frequently asserted that the platform bound him to accept its terms and adhere to its provisions.[20]

The mandate of the Republican party was far from clear, and even had Lincoln attempted to conform to its vague provisions, it would have furnished no practical guide to the political situation which confronted him. There was, in fact, no national Republican party. There were state parties— and it had been state considerations at Chicago that led the delegates to pass over the party's outstanding man and select Lincoln. Andrew Curtin feared he could not be elected

---

[18] *Ibid.,* II, 2–3.
[19] *Ibid.,* III, 390–391. See also *ibid.,* 433–434.
[20] *Ibid.,* IV, 199, 211, 250.

governor of Pennsylvania if Seward were the nominee. Henry S. Lane thought Indiana would vote against him. Richard Yates professed to believe he could not become governor of Illinois on a ticket headed by Seward. Candidate John Andrew of Massachusetts came to Chicago to work against Seward. State, not national, considerations nominated Lincoln; and state parties elected him. Twenty-two of the 33 states had an organized Republican party, and a handful were safely Republican with Republican governors and recently successful organizations full of enthusiasm. In eleven crucial states, three in New England and the others stretching westward to the Mississippi, the Republicans had vigorous gubernatorial candidates. In them the national campaign turned on the state elections. Each went Republican, and in each state, except Massachusetts and Illinois, the governor ran ahead of Lincoln. The Republican party in the states had elected a president for the nation. If Lincoln were to weld a national party, he must first wrest control of its segments from the governors.

Since the governors had elected Lincoln, they had no hesitancy in instructing him on his program. Sewardites and moderates among the politicians counseled moderation and conciliation in the secession crisis. Tentatively, Lincoln experimented with the idea of bringing Southerners, Constitutional Unionists who had supported John Bell and Edward Everett, into his official family. William Cullen Bryant advised it, and Lincoln hoped to bring John A. Gilmer into the cabinet. But the President-elect foresaw the futility of such efforts to mend the sectional breach with patronage plaster. "We could not safely take more than one such man . . . the danger being to lose the confidence of our own friends." His friends, indeed, or a vociferous section of them, favored no conciliation with the South. Old Barnburners assembled in New York to demand that the

abolitionist Salmon P. Chase go into the cabinet. In Indiana
the new governor called for an abolitionist crusade. Early
in January when newly elected governors, the real or titular
heads of the Republican parties, assumed office, they called
for war. John Andrew struck a dramatic note in Massachusetts and found echoing response from Austin Blair in Michigan. Richard Yates instructed his constituent who was
going to the White House to show firmness and wisdom and
to use the military power to defend the Constitution. By
the time of his inauguration, Lincoln had heard the clear
voices of the Republican politicians. The majority of them
would brook no compromise with the South and were arm-
ing their states for coercion.[21]

The insistence of the governors increased after the new
administration began. While Lincoln ignored the governors
in distributing patronage, he could not dismiss their demands for action. The Fort Sumter expedition and the sub-
sequent calls for troops, while not dictated by the governors,
accorded with their demands. Yet, even as he took an action
they demanded, Lincoln seized the initiative from the state
political leaders. In the long run, national decisions had to
be made by national officers, and Lincoln did not shirk the
obligation. As he had advised Zachary Taylor to do, the
president was prepared to say, or seem to say, "By the Eternal, I take the responsibility."

With the initiative in his hands, Lincoln moved to limit
the influence of the governors. When, early in May, the
governors of Western states assembled in Cleveland to urge
the administration to greater action and to outline demands
for marching boldly to the Gulf of Mexico, Lincoln took
them at their word and called for forty regiments of three-

---

21 *Ibid.*, 152, 163, 173; William B. Hesseltine, *Lincoln and the
War Governors* (New York, 1949), 115–135.

year volunteers. These were no state militia called by commanders-in-chief of state troops and loaned temporarily to
the government, but federal soldiers subject to the laws of
the United States. Without knowing it, or even realizing the
political consequences of their acts, the governors raised the
troops and commissioned the officers. But they were no
longer commanders-in-chief; they were convenient recruiting officers for a growing national army. The generals owed
their appointments to the President, and the colonels held
their commissions at his pleasure. Lincoln had taken command.[22]

Thereafter, the President and the federal government
kept the governors busy with new duties. Moreover, to
harass them, and to raise the specter of their loss of power,
the war department authorized colonels to raise regiments
in the states without reference to, and in competition with,
the troops the governors were raising. The governors protested and won their point, but the government turned to
permitting generals to recruit their own commands. John
Andrew saw clearly the political implication of allowing
Benjamin F. Butler to control the regiments he raised. He
squabbled with Butler, and carried his case to Washington.
It was symbolic of the declining power of the governors that
he appealed where once he had directed. It was a greater
symbol when he lost his appeal.

The efforts of the governors to recruit troops brought
them increased difficulties both with the government and
with their own constituents. Steadily they lost influence,
and, with it, much of their political power. John Andrew
and other governors, most of them abolitionists, seized upon

---

[22] William B. Hesseltine and Hazel C. Wolf, "The Cleveland
Conference of 1861," *Ohio Archeological and Historical Society
Quarterly,* LVI (1947), 158–265.

the hope that they could force the administration to use Negro troops and at the same time advance the abolitionist cause. Andrew and others concocted an elaborate scheme— it really grew into the dimensions of a plot—to raise troops for an army to be commanded by Frémont which would set forth without reference to Lincoln's war to invade the South and arm slaves. To mature the plan, Andrew called the governors to a meeting at Altoona, Pennsylvania, on September 23, 1862. It was no coincidence that Lincoln chose the previous day to issue the preliminary Emancipation Proclamation. The proclamation was a masterstroke of politics, cutting the humanitarian ground from under the state politicians, and leaving them with only the alternative of applauding the President's acts.[23]

Thereafter, both the prestige and the power of the governors ebbed. They had lost the power to direct war policy, had lost control of troops as they became recruiting sergeants. Loss of prestige meant loss of political power, and by the elections of 1862 the governors had reason to fear they might be ousted from their offices. Democrats won control of legislatures and put Horatio Seymour in the governor's chair in Albany. But, even as the state politicians were about to succumb to despair, Lincoln moved to their aid. In the border states, he had used the army to control elections and to insure the establishment of loyal governments. In 1863 he moved with arbitrary arrests, soldiers at the polls, and soldiers sent home to vote, into the Northern states. In Ohio, Indiana, and Pennsylvania, troops patrolled the polls and insured the election of Republicans. On November 19, 1863, while Lincoln was speaking at Gettys-

---

[23] William B. Hesseltine and Hazel C. Wolf, "The Altoona Conference and the Emancipation Proclamation," *Pennsylvania Magazine of History and Biography*, LXXI (1948), 195–205.

burg, a regiment was supervising a special congressional election in nearby Delaware. By 1864 the troops were ready for political action. In a sufficient number of states to control the electoral college, the army turned the balance between Lincoln and McClellan. And with Lincoln's victory there went the election of the governors. In 1860 the governors, masters of the party in the states, had put Lincoln in the White House. In 1864 the man in the White House, with mastery over a national party, insured the election of the governors.

Building a national party, however, involved more than subordinating the politicians in the states. There were, in addition, the politicians in Congress, and with them Lincoln faced constantly the hated specter of factionalism. In the Senate were Republicans of long experience in both state and national office. William Pitt Fessenden, Charles Sumner, Henry Wilson, Zachariah Chandler, Jacob Collamer, Lyman Trumbull, Benjamin F. Wade, and John P. Hale had long senatorial service behind them, while David Wilmot, John Sherman, and others had been in the House of Representatives. Two senators from Kansas, James H. Lane and Samuel C. Pomeroy, and two from restored Virginia, John S. Carlile and Waitman Willey, were untried as senators, but fully experienced in the arts of politics. In the House, Galusha Grow, Thaddeus Stevens, John A. Bingham, James M. Ashley, Schuyler Colfax, George W. Julian, Elihu B. Washburn, Owen Lovejoy, and Justin Morrill were well-known and time-tested politicians.[24] They were superior in experience to Abraham Lincoln, who, as Sam Medary saw it, "most unfortunately for the country and his party, had never progressed farther in statesmanship than is

---

[24] James G. Blaine, *Twenty Years of Congress* (Norwich, Conn., 1884–1886), I, 316–319.

learned in the pleasant position of county court practice where wit and wisdom reign more for the amusement of the thing than to *settle* great state questions."[25]

With such political talent in Congress, Lincoln made no effort to assume leadership in legislation. He had, indeed, no legislative program to promote, and faced none of the problems of the legislative leader who needed to bargain and cajole, to coerce and to compromise to get support for a bill. On the other hand, he had a war to conduct and needed the support of an integrated national party to bring it to a successful conclusion. But here he met discordant factions, differing from one another on the purpose of the war, the manner in which it should be fought, and the results to be obtained. Here he met Conciliators who would bargain with the South, Moderates who wished to conduct the war with as little social and economic disturbance as possible, and Radicals who wished to effect a drastic reorganization of American society at its end.

Fully aware of the contending factions, Lincoln delayed calling Congress into session until four months after his inauguration. Democrats charged then, and the echo has reverberated for a century, that Lincoln precipitated a war in order to save and consolidate the Republican party. Whatever his purpose, his act gave the party a program and brought conciliators and compromisers among the politicians into line. Moreover, as the people of the North rushed to the mass meetings—and some to the regiments—the politicians could read the signs. "Mr. Lincoln judged wisely" in delaying the assembling of Congress, thought James G. Blaine. "Time was needed for the growth and consolidation of Northern opinion, and that senators and representatives, after the full development of patriotic feeling in the free

---

[25] Columbus *Crisis*, April 11, 1861.

states, would meet in a frame of mind better suited to the discharge of the weighty duties devolving upon them."[26]

In addition to the desire to use public pressure on the politicians, Lincoln had, in Blaine's opinion, another reason for delaying the assembling of Congress. Kentucky's congressmen had not yet been chosen, and the President desired to "give ample time for canvassing" for the special election on June 20. In the canvass, recounted Blaine, Lincoln "did everything therefore that he could properly do, to aid Kentucky in reaching a conclusion favorable to the Union." In the view of Democrats, who used none of Blaine's mealymouthed verbosity to describe the situation, Lincoln went beyond the bounds of propriety in aiding Kentucky. General Jeremiah T. Boyle arrested citizens on the eve of election, and troops at the polls discouraged Democratic voters. The results were heartening to Lincoln. Nine out of Kentucky's ten congressmen were Unionists who could be grateful to Lincoln for their success.

The combination of popular pressure and direct aid, illustrated in the first months of the administration, frequently proved an effective device for dealing with the politicians in Congress. It was not, however, always available to Lincoln. The Radical faction, too, used the Union Leagues and the propaganda agencies of the Union League clubs to build up popular pressure for their policies. Moreover, the Radicals controlled the congressional Committee on the Conduct of the War which was at once an investigating body, a fountain-head of Radical propaganda, and a pressure group seeking to direct war policy.

With these factional groups Lincoln had to deal. Frequently he found himself forced to yield. Whatever the military merits of George B. McClellan may have been,

---

[26] Blaine, *Twenty Years of Congress,* I, 309.

political necessity demanded his removal from command. Less able and less successful generals—Benjamin Butler and Nathaniel Banks, for example—whose political views were more acceptable to the vociferous Radical clique, remained long in command. Whatever the humanitarian or diplomatic advantages of the Emancipation Proclamation may have been, its issuance and its timing constituted a yielding to the politicians in state and national capitols.

Yet, Abraham Lincoln was not the pliant tool of the Radical faction. He yielded to political necessity, but he was apt in evading the demands of the politicians and ingenious in diverting them. He handled the Chase-Seward imbroglio in his cabinet with dexterity, took advantage of the premature announcement of Chase's hopes in the Pomeroy Circular, and released Chase from his cabinet after the political danger was passed. He used state legislators and Montgomery Blair's corps of postmasters to launch a "grass roots" demand for his own renomination. He bargained for Frémont's removal during the campaign of 1864. He was a master politician, using the patronage, the army, the ability to appeal to the people over the heads of the politicians, and a shrewd capacity to bargain to build a national party and to keep rival politicians from open and overt revolt.

His most serious problem and his nearest defeat had to do with the issues of Reconstruction. His plans were many, and each was political in orientation and looked to the eventual establishment of proper practical relations between the seceded states and the national government. Beginning with the border states, where Lincoln fostered Unionist parties and encouraged the replacement of disloyal governors, his program developed through the establishment of military governors to the eventual announcement of a full-blown Proclamation of Amnesty and Reconstruction. From the beginning, Democratic critics pointed out that Lincoln's plans were political and designed to create a personal party, supported by the army. In the opinion of the Columbus *Crisis*, all of Lincoln's acts revealed "settled designs upon the rights of the states and the liberties of the people."[27] Certainly, Lincoln had no program for restoring the old rights of the states or of restoring the *old* Federal Union. He was waging a war against the states, and was building a national party. He watched patiently while Andrew Johnson labored in Tennessee to create a political party before he tried to restore the machinery of government. He gave free reign to Butler and Banks in New Orleans as they sought for a loyal nucleus about which to gather a party.

When Lincoln issued his proclamation of Amnesty and Reconstruction in December, 1863, the Democrats were quick to see its political significance. "As a party manifesto," pronounced the New York *World*, "it is a creditable specimen of political dexterity. It trims with marvelous dexterity between the two factions of the Republican party." It was, in fact, "Mr. Lincoln's trump card for the presidential nomination." Other Democrats were more apt in spelling out the details, and soon they were counting the number of voters who would be needed to carry the states of the South. The movement, said the *World*, was not "discreditable to Mr. Lincoln's shrewdness as a politician. . . . There could not be a shrewder device for enabling President Lincoln to re-elect himself." The one-tenth who would take the "abolition oath" would cast the electoral votes of the Southern states. When a military expedition went off to Florida, the *World* saw the movement as not military but political: "The object was to make it a rotten-borough state under the amnesty proclamation, so that it could throw its electoral vote for Mr. Lincoln."[28]

---

[27] Columbus *Crisis*, August 8, 1861.
[28] New York *World*, December 10, 1863.

The Radical politicians of Congress hardly needed instruction from the Democrats on the political meaning of the amnesty proclamation. Long had they favored a program of conquest which would insure far-reaching social and economic changes in the South. They approved Ben Butler's harsh regime in New Orleans as they saw him destroying the Southern economic system and organizing a new electorate. They approved the social experiments in the Sea Islands of Carolina where the army, treasury officials, and agents of humanitarian societies quarreled with each other as they sought to combine a reorganization of society with the production of cotton. They saw, as quickly as the Democrats, that Lincoln's plans embodied his personal control over the Southern states. When congressmen from a reconstructed government in Arkansas arrived in Washington, Radical Henry Winter Davis denounced Lincoln's proclamation as "a grave usurpation upon the legislative authority of the people." Soon Davis had ready a bill for a more complicated process of Reconstruction than Lincoln contemplated, and the members of Congress turned to denouncing Lincoln and his schemes. In the Senate, where Reconstruction policies were a constant subject of debate, the Davis bill received little specific attention. The final passage of the Wade-Davis Bill was done with so little enthusiasm that Lincoln had no hesitancy in giving it a pocket veto and accompanying it with a fresh declaration of his own policy.

Radicals Wade and Davis issued a "manifesto" denouncing presidential usurpation, and thereafter, until the end of his life, the Radical politicians harassed Lincoln on the issues of Reconstruction. The election of 1864 brought success to the Republicans without recourse to the electoral votes of the "rotten-borough" states, and in the congressional session of 1864–1865 Charles Sumner filibustered against the recognition of a reconstructed government in Louisiana. On the issue, Lincoln was forced to retreat, and he spent his last weeks devising new schemes of Reconstruction. The new schemes never matured, and Andrew Johnson inherited the problem and faced the determined and well-organized politicians of Congress.

The end was inconclusive. Lincoln had, indeed, built a national party. He had used the patronage, the prestige of his position, the army, and skillful popular appeals to subordinate the state parties and mold them into national unity. He had had less success in combatting factionalism at the national level, had not succeeded in winning undisputed control over the party he had created. He might, indeed, have recalled his early definition of politicians as "a set of men who have interests aside from the interests of the people, and who, to say the most of them, are, taken as a mass, at least one long step removed from honest men." And, had he remembered this, he might also have recalled, as he surveyed his own substantial accomplishments, that he had also added—"being a politician myself . . . ."

BIBLIOGRAPHY

THIS bibliography is based on a list which Professor Hesseltine kept through the years for his own use, a copy of which is available in the State Historical Society of Wisconsin. The list of books is complete. The list of articles omits contributions to encyclopedias, articles written under pseudonyms, and a few fugitive pieces for which little or no bibliographical information could be found. The book reviews are limited to those published in the four professional journals for which Professor Hesseltine wrote most regularly: *The American Historical Review, The Journal of Southern History, The Wisconsin Magazine of History,* and *The Mississippi Valley Historical Review* (now *The Journal of American History*).

The editor wishes to thank Mrs. Jeanne Delgado, who compiled and edited this bibliography, and Mrs. William B. Hesseltine, who graciously assisted in checking it.

BOOKS

Civil War Prisons: A Study in War Psychology. Columbus: Ohio State University Press, 1930. (Studies and Contributions in History and Political Science, No. 12.)

Ulysses S. Grant, Politician. New York: Dodd, Mead and Co., 1935. Reprinted. New York: Frederick Unger, 1957. (American Classics series.)

A History of the South, 1607–1936. New York: Prentice-Hall, 1936.

A Syllabus of United States History. Madison: University of Wisconsin Press, 1940. Rev. Ed., 1955.

The South in American History. New York: Prentice-Hall, 1943. [First published as *A History of the South, 1607–1936.* New York: Prentice-Hall, 1936.] Second Edition, with David Smiley. Englecliffs: Prentice-Hall, 1960.

Lincoln and the War Governors. New York: Alfred A. Knopf, 1948.

The Rise and Fall of Third Parties, From Anti-Masonry to Wallace.
Washington: Public Affairs Press, 1948. Reprinted. Gloucester:
Peter Smith, 1957.

Confederate Leaders in the New South. Baton Rouge: Louisiana
State University Press, 1950. (Walter Lynwood Fleming Lectures
in Southern History, Louisiana State University.)

Pioneer's Mission: The Story of Lyman C. Draper. Madison: State
Historical Society of Wisconsin, 1954.

Editor. *Dr. J. G. M. Ramsey: Autobiography and Letters.* Nashville:
Tennessee Historical Commission, 1954.

Editor, with Donald R. McNeil. *In Support of Clio: Essays in
Memory of Herbert A. Kellar.* Madison: State Historical Society
of Wisconsin, 1958.

Abraham Lincoln: Architect of the Nation. Fort Wayne: Allen
County-Fort Wayne Historical Society, 1959.

Lincoln's Plan of Reconstruction. Tuscaloosa: Confederate Publishing Company, 1960. (Confederate Centennial Studies, No. 13.)

Editor. *Three Against Lincoln: Murat Halstead Reports the Cau-
cuses of 1860.* Baton Rouge: Louisiana State University Press,
1960.

With Hazel Wolf. *The Blue and the Gray on the Nile.* Chicago:
University of Chicago Press, 1961.

Editor, with Rex G. Fisher. *Trimmers, Trucklers and Temporizers:
Notes of Murat Halstead From the Political Conventions of 1856.*
Madison: State Historical Society of Wisconsin, 1961.

Editor. *The Tragic Conflict: The Civil War and Reconstruction.*
New York: George Braziller, 1962.

Third Party Movements in the United States. Princeton: D. Van
Nostrand Co., 1962.

ARTICLES

"Arkansas Note: Trial of Speaker Hill." *Southwest Political and
Social Science Quarterly,* 6: 276–277 (December, 1925).

"Military Prisons of St. Louis, 1861–1865." *Missouri Historical
Review,* 23: 380–399 (April, 1929).

"The Underground Railroad from Confederate Prisons to East
Tennessee." *East Tennessee Historical Society Publication,* 1:
55–69 (1930).

"Methodism and Reconstruction in East Tennessee." *East Tennessee Historical Society Publications*, 3: 42–61 (January, 1931).

"Tennessee's Invitation to Carpetbaggers." *East Tennessee Historical Society Publications*, 4: 102–115 (January, 1932).

"The Propaganda Literature of Confederate Prisons." *Journal of Southern History*, 1: 56–66 (February, 1935).

"Economic Factors in the Abandonment of Reconstruction." *Mississippi Valley Historical Review*, 22: 191–210 (September, 1935).

"Some New Aspects of the Pro-Slavery Argument." *Journal of Negro History*, 21: 1–14 (January, 1936).

"A Quarter-Century of the Association for the Study of Negro Life and History." *Journal of Negro History*, 25: 440–449 (October, 1940).

"The Librarians and the Footnotes." *Wilson Library Bulletin*, 15: 762–764 (May, 1941).

With Louis Kaplan. "Doctors of Philosophy in History: A Statistical Study." *American Historical Review*, 47: 765–800 (July, 1942).

With Louis Kaplan. "Negro Doctors of Philosophy in History." *Negro History Bulletin*, 6: 59, 67 (December, 1942).

With Louis Kaplan. "Woman Doctors of Philosophy in History." *Journal of Higher Education*, 14: 254–259 (May, 1943).

"The Post-War Political Order." *Fellowship*, 9: 103–105 (June, 1943).

"History for the Common Man." *New Leader*, 26: 5, 6 (June 5, 1943).

"A Lesson from American History: War and Unconditional Surrender." *New Leader*, 26: 4, 7 (August 21, 1943).

"Gustavus Myers: Muckraker in History." *Progressive*, 7: 8 (August 30, 1943).

"The Pryor-Potter Duel." *Wisconsin Magazine of History*, 27: 400–409 (June, 1944).

"Shall We Abolish the State Department?" *Progressive*, 7: 1, 11 (October 4, 1943).

"The New Federalist: Beard and the Constitution." *New Leader*, 26: 5, 7 (November 20, 1943).

"The Abdication of the Supreme Court." *Progressive*, 8: 4 (January 31, 1944).

"Regions, Classes and Sections in American History." *Journal of Land and Public Utility Economics*, 20: 35–44 (February, 1944).

"With Malice Toward None." *Progressive*, 8: 4 (March 20, 1944).

"Policing for Peace or Profits?" *Progressive*, 8: 4 (April 3, 1944).

"Harvest of Hate." *Progressive*, 8: 4 (April 17, 1944).

"Beware a Global Gestapo!" *Progressive*, 8: 4 (May 1, 1944).

"The History-Teaching Controversy: Requiem and Resume." *New Leader*, 27: 5 (June 17, 1944).

"Salvaging the War's Mental Wrecks." *Progressive*, 8: 4 (July 17, 1944).

"How American Soldiers Voted Last Time." *Progressive*, 8: 5 (October 16, 1944).

"Who's That Knocking at Our Door?" *Progressive*, 8: 4 (October 30, 1944).

"Hollywoodrow Wilson." *Progressive*, 8: 8 (December 4, 1944).

"What's Behind the Drive for Finding War Criminals." *Call*, 12: 5 (March 19, 1945).

"Atrocities—Then and Now." *Progressive*, 9: 4 (May 7, 1945).

"Brass Hats Never Learn." *Progressive*, 9: 4 (June 18, 1945).

"Britain's Future." *Progressive*, 9: 4, 11 (September 24, 1945).

"Britain Looks to America." *Progressive*, 9: 4 (October 1, 1945).

"Civilities in the Civil War." *Progressive*, 9: 8, 12 (November 12, 1945).

"Bryan—Twenty Years After." *Progressive*, 9: 5, 11 (December 3, 1945).

"Britain's Languid Labor Government." *Progressive*, 10: 4, 10 (January 28, 1946).

"An Open in England." *Progressive*, 10: 7, 15 (February 11, 1946).

"Test Demonstration of Democracy." *Progressive*, 10: 4, 11 (June 24, 1946).

With Hazel Wolf. "The New England Governors vs. Lincoln: The Providence Conference." *Rhode Island History*, 5: 105–112 (October, 1946).

"Stalincrat in Milwaukee." *New Leader*, 29: 4 (October 26, 1946).

"Lincoln's War Governors." *Abraham Lincoln Quarterly,* 4: 153–200 (December, 1946), 153–200.

"Lincoln: New Books and Old Letters." *Progressive,* 11: 9 (February 10, 1947).

"History Roller Coaster." *Motive,* 7: 5–6 (March, 1947).

"Two Years Afterwards." *Progressive,* 11: 1–2 (May 12, 1947).

"Third Parties: Instruments of American Politics." *Progressive,* 11: 1–2 (June 30, 1947).

With Hazel Wolf. "The Altoona Conference and the Emancipation Proclamation." *Pennsylvania Magazine of History and Biography,* 71: 195–205 (July, 1947).

With Hazel Wolf. "The Cleveland Conference of 1861." *Ohio State Archeological and Historical Quarterly,* 56: 258–266 (July, 1947).

"The Failure of the New Deal." *Progressive,* 11: 5, 11 (July 7, 1947).

"The New Deal and the Progressive Tradition." *Progressive,* 11: 4 (July 21, 1947).

"Republicans Once Were Liberal." *Progressive,* 11: 4, 10, 11 (July 28, 1947).

"The GOP: Loyal Opposition." *Progressive,* 11: 4, 11 (August 4, 1947).

"Third Parties: Their Emergence in the Nineteenth Century," *Progressive,* 11: 4, 11 (August 11, 1947).

"Bull Mooses and the Great Betrayal." *Progressive,* 11: 4, 12 (August 18, 1947).

"The Progressives of 1924." *Progressive,* 11: 4 (August 25, 1947).

"What's the Matter with the Socialists?" *Progressive,* 11: 4, 11 (September 1, 1947).

"American Labor's Satellite Parties." *Progressive,* 11: 4 (September 8, 1947).

"Instruments of the Agrarian Revolt." *Progressive,* 11: 4 (September 15, 1947).

"Handicaps for a New Party." *Progressive,* 11: 4 (September 22, 1947).

"Philosophical Obstacles to Action." *Progressive,* 11: 4, 8 (September 29, 1947).

With Hazel Wolf. "Kentucky's Last Peace Effort." *Register of Kentucky History,* 45: 335–339 (October, 1947).

"Robert Marion La Follette and the Principles of Americanism." *Wisconsin Magazine of History*, 31: 261–267 (March, 1948).

"Is There a Bryan in your Barn?" *Progressive*, 12: 20–22 (May, 1948).

"The Value of Regional History." *Arkansas Historical Quarterly*, 7: 11–19 (Spring, 1948).

"The Perversion of Progressivism." *Progressive*, 12: 5–8 (September, 1948).

With Hazel Wolf. "Lincoln, the Governors, and States Rights." *Social Studies*, 39: 350–355 (December, 1948).

"The Society and the Historian." In *The State Historical Society of Wisconsin: A Century of Service* (Madison: State Historical Society of Wisconsin, 1948. Pp. 23–31).

"Andersonville." *Georgia Review*, 3: 103–114 (Spring, 1949).

With Larry Gara. "Arkansas' Confederate Leaders after the War." *Arkansas Historical Quarterly*, 9: 259–269 (Winter, 1950).

With Larry Gara. "Confederate Leaders in Post-War Alabama." *Alabama Review*, 4: 5–22 (January, 1951).

With Larry Gara. "Georgia's Confederate Leaders after Appomattox." *Georgia Historical Quarterly*, 35: 1–15 (March, 1951).

With Larry Gara. "Mississippi's Confederate Leaders after the War." *Journal of Mississippi History*, 13: 88–100 (April, 1951).

"Introduction" to Part II. In Merrill Jensen, ed., *Regionalism in America* (Madison: University of Wisconsin Press, 1951. Pp. 143–145).

"Lyman Copeland Draper, 1815–1891." *Wisconsin Magazine of History*, 35: 163–166, 231–234 (Spring, 1952).

Editor. "A Glimpse of Waiilatpu, 1839." *Oregon Historical Quarterly*, 53: 192–196 (September, 1952).

"Lincoln's Problems in Wisconsin." *Lincoln Fellowship of Wisconsin*, Historical Bulletin, No. 10 (1952). Reprinted: *Wisconsin Magazine of History*, 48: 187–195 (Spring, 1965).

Editor, with Larry Gara. "Andrew H. Ernst, Pioneer Horticulturalist." *Bulletin of the Historical and Philosophical Society of Ohio*, 11: 37–41 (January, 1953).

"Lyman C. Draper and the South." *Journal of Southern History*, 19: 20–31 (February, 1953).

With Larry Gara. "Superintendent Draper and Wisconsin Journal of Education." *Wisconsin Journal of Education*, 85: 23–25 (March, 1953).

With Larry Gara. "Lyman C. Draper, Superintendent of Public Instruction." *Wisconsin Journal of Education*, 85: 10 (April, 1953).

Editor, with Larry Gara. "Postwar Problems of a Virginia Historian." *Virginia Magazine of History and Biography*, 61: 193–195 (April, 1953).

"The Mississippi Career of Lyman C. Draper." *Journal of Mississippi History*, 15: 165–180 (July, 1953).

"Lyman C. Draper and Alabama." *Alabama Review*, 6: 191–197 (July, 1953).

Editor, with Larry Gara. "Lyman Draper's Account of Lost Western Manuscripts." *Bulletin of the Historical and Philosophical Society of Ohio*, 11: 192–204 (July, 1953).

With Larry Gara. "Draper: Historian Turned Educator." *Mid-America*, 35: 131–143 [new series 24] (July, 1953).

Editor, with Larry Gara. "The Archives of Pennsylvania: A Glimpse at an Editor's Problems." *Pennsylvania Magazine of History and Biography*, 77: 328–331 (July, 1953).

"The Return of the Louisiana Documents." *Library Quarterly*, 23: 284–286 (October, 1953).

"Lyman Draper at Granville College." *Denison Alumnus*, 45: 12–14 (October, 1953).

Editor, with Larry Gara. "The Historical Fraternity: Correspondence of Historians Grigsby, Henry, and Draper." *Virginia Magazine of History and Biography*, 61: 450–471 (October, 1953).

Editor, with Larry Gara. "Lyman C. Draper and the Shane Papers." *Filson Club Quarterly*, 27: 327–333 (October, 1953).

Editor, with Larry Gara. "Across Georgia and into Alabama, 1817–1818." *Georgia Historical Quarterly*, 37: 329–340 (December, 1953).

With Henry Ewbank, Jr. "Old Voices in the New South." *Quarterly Journal of Speech*, 39: 451–458 (December, 1953).

"History Begins at Home." *Historical Messenger of the Milwaukee County Historical Society*, 10: 2–4 (March, 1954).

Editor, with Larry Gara. "A Visit to Kinderhook." *New York History*, 35: 177–184 (April, 1954).

"Lyman C. Draper and the Wisconsin Academy of Science." *Wisconsin Academy Review*, 1: 1–3 (Spring, 1954).

With Larry Gara. "History Publishing in 1849." *The Historian*, 16: 135–141 (Spring, 1954).

"Andersonville Revisited." *Georgia Review*, 10: 92–100 (Spring, 1956).

Editor, with Larry Gara. "Letters of A. Randall to Lyman Copeland Draper, 1846–1855." *Bulletin of the Historical and Philosophical Society of Ohio*, 15: 141–152 (April, 1957).

"Coercion in American Life." *Liberation*, 2: 12, 19 (November, 1957).

"The Civil War Industry." *Michigan History*, 42: 421–434 (December, 1958).

"A Word to the Wise." In Clifford L. Lord, ed., *Ideas in Conflict: A Colloquium On Certain Problems in Historical Society in the United States and Canada* (Harrisburg: American Association for State and Local History, 1958. Pp. 9–15).

Editor. "A Confederate Sailor's Lament." *Civil War History*, 5: 99–102 (March, 1959).

"The Phenomenon of American Political Parties." *Pakiston Horizon*, 12: 215–220 (September, 1959).

"Introduction." In Howard P. Nash, *Third Parties in American Politics* (Washington: Public Affairs Press, 1959. Pp. v–vi).

"The Challenge of the Artifact." In James H. Rodabaugh, comp. and ed., *The Present World of History: A Conference on Certain Problems in Historical Agency Work in the United States* (Madison: American Association for State and Local History, 1959. Pp. 64–70).

"Hot Lights and Cold Tea: Correspondence of William B. Hesseltine and Donald R. McNeil to Forrest H. Sweet, June 7, July 28, August 11, 1958." *Manuscripts*, 12: 26–33 (Winter, 1960).

"Sectionalism and Regionalism in American History." *Journal of Southern History*, 26: 25–34 (February, 1960).

"Abraham Lincoln and the Politicians." *Civil War History*, 6: 43–55 (March, 1960).

Editor. " 'Douglas, Deadlock, and Disunion,' by Murat Halstead." *American Heritage*, 11: 56–59, 80–87 (June, 1960).

"Lincoln's Plan for Reconstruction." In Ralph G. Newman, *Lincoln for the Ages* (Garden City: Doubleday, 1960, Pp. 372–377).

"Four American Traditions." *Journal of Southern History,* 27: 3–32 (February, 1961).

"Speech and History." *Central States Speech Journal,* 12: 176–181 (Spring, 1961).

"Civil War Boom." *Progressive,* 25: 15–16 (May, 1961).

"Ramsey and Draper vs. Bancroft: History for the Common Man," *East Tennessee Historical Society Publications,* 33: 3–16 (1961).

"Foreword." In Robert Gray Gunderson, *Old Gentlemen's Convention: The Washington Peace Conference of 1861* (Madison: University of Wisconsin Press, 1961. Pp. v–viii).

"Lincoln's Concept of the National Purpose." In *The National Purpose: A Symposium. Bulletin of the Institute for American Studies of New Mexico Highlands University* (Las Vegas: Institute for American Studies of New Mexico Highlands University, 1961).

With Hazel Wolf. "A Civil War Veteran in Central Africa." *Midway: A Magazine of Discovery in the Arts and Sciences,* 9: 38–57 (January 1962).

"Civil War Prisons—Introduction." *Civil War History,* 8: 117–120 (June, 1962).

BOOK REVIEWS

Abraham Lincoln Association Papers Delivered Before the Members of the Abraham Lincoln Association, in *Mississippi Valley Historical Review,* 21: 281 (September, 1934).

Adams, James Truslow, *America's Tragedy,* in *Mississippi Valley Historical Review,* 21: 565–566 (March, 1935).

Baringer, William E., *A House Dividing: Lincoln as President Elect,* in *Mississippi Valley Historical Review,* 32: 449 (December, 1945).

Barker, Alan, *The Civil War in America,* in *Mississippi Valley Historical Review,* 48: 707–708 (March, 1962).

Basso, Hamilton, *Beauregard: The Great Creole,* in *Mississippi Valley Historical Review,* 20: 422–423 (December, 1933).

Bill, Alfred Hoyt, *The Beleaguered City: Richmond, 1861–1865,* in *Mississippi Valley Historical Review,* 33: 167 (June, 1946).

Blied, Reverend Benjamin J., *Catholic Aspects of the War for Independence, The War of 1812, The War with Mexico, The War with Spain,* in *Wisconsin Magazine of History,* 34: 122 (Winter, 1950).

Boatner, Mark Mayo, III, *The Civil War Dictionary,* in *Wisconsin Magazine of History,* 44: 138–139 (Winter, 1960–1961).

Bragg, Jefferson Davis, *Louisiana in the Confederacy,* in *Mississippi Valley Historical Review,* 29: 105–106 (June, 1942).

Brewton, William W., *The Son of Thunder,* in *Mississippi Valley Historical Review,* 23: 574–575 (March, 1937).

Brooks, William E., *Grant of Appomattox: A Study of the Man,* in *American Historical Review,* 48: 658–659 (April, 1943).

Bruce, Robert V., *Lincoln and the Tools of War,* in *Journal of Southern History,* 22: 525–526 (November, 1956).

Buck, Paul H., *The Road to Reunion: 1865–1900,* in *Mississippi Valley Historical Review,* 24: 264–265 (September, 1937).

Bullard, F. Lauriston, *Abraham Lincoln and the Widow Bixby,* in *Wisconsin Magazine of History,* 30: 483–484 (June, 1947).

Catton, Bruce, *A Stillness at Appomattox,* in *American Historical Review,* 59: 727 (April, 1954).

Catton, Bruce, *The American Heritage,* in *Wisconsin Magazine of History,* 38: 178–180 (Spring, 1955).

Clark, Thomas D., *Pills, Petticoats and Plows: The Southern Country Store,* in *Mississippi Valley Historical Review,* 31: 281 (September, 1944).

Coleman, Charles H., *The Election of 1868: The Democratic Effort to Regain Control,* in *Mississippi Valley Historical Review,* 21: 101–102 (June, 1934).

Cotterill, R. S., *The Old South. The Geographic, Economic, Social, Political, and Cultural Expansion, Institutions, and Nationalism of the Ante-Bellum South,* in *Mississippi Valley Historical Review,* 23: 412–413 (December, 1936).

Coulter, E. Merton, ed., *The Course of the South to Secession. An Interpretation by Ulrich Bonnell Phillips,* in *Mississippi Valley Historical Review,* 27: 298–299 (September, 1940).

Cunamins, Cedric C., *Indiana Public Opinion and the World War, 1914–1917,* in *Wisconsin Magazine of History,* 30: 102 (September, 1946).

De Voto, Bernard, *Year of Decision: 1848,* in *Wisconsin Magazine of History,* 27: 97–98 (September, 1943).

Dick, Everett, *The Dixie Frontier. A Social History of the Southern Frontier from the First Transmontane Beginnings to the Civil War,* in *Wisconsin Magazine of History,* 32: 213 (December, 1948).

Dollard, John, *Caste and Class in a Southern Town,* in *Mississippi Valley Historical Review,* 25: 121 (June, 1938).

Donald, David, *Lincoln Reconsidered: Essays on the Civil War Era,* in *Mississippi Valley Historical Review,* 43: 494 (December, 1956).

Eckenrode, H. J., assisted by Pocahontos Wilson Wright, *Rutherford B. Hayes: Statesman of Reunion,* in *Mississippi Valley Historical Review,* 17: 637–638 (March, 1931).

Eisenschiml, Otto, *The Story of Shiloh,* in *Wisconsin Magazine of History,* 30: 105 (September, 1946).

Eisenschiml, Otto, and E. B. Long, *As Luck Would Have It,* in *Mississippi Valley Historical Review,* 35: 690–691 (March, 1949).

Eisenschiml, Otto, and Ralph Newman, *The American Iliad: The Epic Story of the Civil War as Narrated by Eyewitnesses and Contemporaries,* in *Wisconsin Magazine of History,* 31: 475 (June, 1948).

Franklin, John Hope, *From Slavery to Freedom: A History of American Negroes,* in *American Historical Review,* 54: 155–156 (October, 1948).

Franklin, John Hope, *The Emancipation Proclamation,* in *Journal of Southern History,* 29: 531–532 (November, 1963).

Fuller, J. F. C., *Grant and Lee: A Study in Personality and Generalship,* in *Journal of Southern History,* 1:404–405 (August, 1935).

Govan, Gilbert and James W. Livingood, *The Chattanooga Country, 1540–1951,* in *Wisconsin Magazine of History,* 37: 40–41 (Autumn, 1953).

Green, Homer, *General Grant's Land Stand: A Biography,* in *Mississippi Valley Historical Review,* 23: 580–581 (March, 1937).

Hamilton, Holman, *Zachary Taylor, Soldier of the Republic,* in *Wisconsin Magazine of History,* 25: 361–362 (March, 1942).

Hanry, Robert S., *The Story of Reconstruction,* in *Mississippi Valley Historical Review,* 25: 119 (June, 1938).

Hofstadter, Richard, *The Age of Reform from Bryan to F.D.R.,* in *Wisconsin Magazine of History,* 39: 280 (Summer, 1956).

Howe, Mark De Wolfe, *Touched With Fire: Civil War Letters and Diary of Oliver Wendell Holmes,* in *American Historical Review,* 53: 629 (April, 1948).

Johnson, Charles S., *The Negro College Graduate,* in *Journal of Southern History,* 4: 539–540 (November, 1938).

Jaquette, Henrietta Stratton, ed., *South After Gettysburg: Letters of Cornelia Hancock, 1863–1868,* in *Wisconsin Magazine of History,* 41: 54–56 (Autumn, 1957).

Kann, Samuel R., *The Civil War Career of Thomas A. Scott,* in *Mississippi Valley Historical Review,* 27: 481–482 (December, 1940).

Key, V. O., Jr., with the assistance of Alexander Heard, *Southern Politics in State and Nation,* in *American Historical Review,* 55: 939–941 (July, 1950).

Kroll, Harry H., *I Was a Share-Cropper,* in *Mississippi Valley Historical Review,* 24: 569 (March, 1938).

Lewis, Lloyd, *Captain Sam Grant,* in *Wisconsin Magazine of History,* 34: 220–221 (Summer, 1951).

Lewis, Lloyd, *Sherman, Fighting Prophet,* in *Mississippi Valley Historical Review,* 20: 126 (June, 1933).

Macartney, Clarence E., *Grant and His Generals,* in *Wisconsin Magazine of History,* 37: 115–116 (Winter, 1953–1954).

McKitrick, Eric L., *Andrew Johnson and Reconstruction,* in *Journal of Southern History,* 27: 110–111 (February, 1961).

Monica, Sister Mary, *The Cross in the Wilderness: A Biography of Pioneer Ohio,* in *Mississippi Valley Historical Review,* 18: 132–133 (June, 1931).

Myers, William Starr, *General George Brinton McClellan: A Study in Personality,* in *Mississippi Valley Historical Review,* 21: 564–565 (March, 1935).

Nicolay, Helen, *Lincoln's Secretary. A Biography of John G. Nicolay,* in *Wisconsin Magazine of History,* 34: 113–114 (Winter, 1950).

O'Connor, Richard, *Sheridan the Inevitable,* in *American Historical Review,* 59: 452–453 (January, 1954).

Odum, Howard W., and Harry E. Moore, *American Regionalism: A Cultural-Historical Approach to National Integration,* in *Mississippi Valley Historical Review,* 25: 588–589 (March, 1939).

Osterweis, Rollin G., *Romanticism and Nationalism in the Old South,* in *Mississippi Valley Historical Review,* 36: 516–517 (December, 1949).

Parker, Donald Dean, *Local History: How to Gather It, Write It, and Publish It,* rev. and ed. by Bertha A. Josephson, in *Wisconsin Magazine of History,* 28: 351–352 (March, 1945).

Patton, James Welch, *Unionism and Reconstruction in Tennessee, 1860–1869,* in *Mississippi Valley Historical Review,* 21: 100–101 (June, 1934).

Pratt, Fletcher, *Stanton: Lincoln's Secretary of War,* in *Journal of Southern History,* 20: 272–273 (May, 1954).

Prucha, Francis Paul, *Broadax and Bayonet: The Role of the United States Army in the Development of the Northwest, 1815–1860,* in *Wisconsin Magazine of History,* 36: 267–268 (Summer, 1953).

Randall, J. G., *Constitutional Problems under Lincoln,* in *Journal of Southern History,* 17: 266–267 (May, 1951).

Randall, James G., *The Diary of Orville Hickman Browning, Vol. II,* in *Mississippi Valley Historical Review,* 20: 423–424 (December, 1933).

Raper, Arthur F., *Preface to Peasantry: A Tale of Two Black Belt Counties,* in *Mississippi Valley Historical Review,* 24: 99–100 (June, 1937).

Riddle, Donald W., *Lincoln Runs for Congress,* in *Mississippi Valley Historical Review,* 35: 513–514 (December, 1948).

Robinson, William M., Jr., *Justice in Grey: A History of the Judicial System of the Confederate States of America,* in *Mississippi Valley Historical Review,* 28: 269–270 (September, 1941).

Roland, Charles P., *The Confederacy,* in *Wisconsin Magazine of History,* 44: 138–139 (Winter, 1960–1961).

Sherwin, Oscar, *Prophet of Liberty: The Life and Times of Wendell Phillips,* in *Journal of Southern History,* 24: 511–512 (November, 1958).

Smith, Albert W., *Ezra Cornell: A Character Study,* in *Mississippi Valley Historical Review,* 22: 591 (March, 1936).

Starr, Louis M., *Bohemian Brigade: Civil War Newsmen in Action,* in *American Historical Review,* 60: 687–688 (April, 1955).

Stephenson, George M., *American History Since 1865,* in *American Historical Review,* 45: 237 (October, 1939).

Thomas, Benjamin P., ed., *Three Years with Grant as Recalled by War Correspondent Sylvanus Cadwallader*, in *Mississippi Valley Historical Review*, 42: 759–760 (March, 1956).

Twelve Southerners, *I'll Take My Stand: The South and the Agrarian Tradition*, in *Sewanee Review*, 39: 97–103 (January-March, 1931).

Walton, John, *John Filson of Kentucke*, in *American Historical Review*, 62: 491 (January, 1957).

Williams, Kenneth P., *Lincoln Finds A General: A Military Study of the Civil War, Vol. III*, in *American Historical Review*, 58: 651–652 (April, 1953).

Williams, Kenneth P., *Lincoln Finds A General: A Military Study of the Civil War, Vol. IV*, in *American Historical Review*, 62: 1009–1010 (July, 1957).

Woodson, Carter G., *The Negro in Our History*, in *Journal of Southern History*, 7: 419–420 (August, 1941).

Woodward, C. Vann, *Origins of the New South, 1877–1913*, in *American Historical Review*, 57: 993–994 (July, 1952).

Yearns, Wilfred Buck, *The Confederate Congress*, in *American Historical Review*, 66: 757–758 (April, 1961).

APPENDIX

*Students Earning the Doctorate under
William B. Hesseltine's Direction*

1934

GEORGE F. GRANT

1937

T. HARRY WILLIAMS

1938

MARY RULKOTTER (DEARING)

1939

GEORGE WINSTON SMITH

1940

RICHARD N. CURRENT
BENJAMIN A. QUARLES
E. BRUCE THOMPSON

1942

FRANK FREIDEL
HORACE S. MERRILL
KENNETH M. STAMPP

1946

FRANK L. KLEMENT

1947

GEORGE R. WOOLFOLK

1948

ROBERT J. RAYBACK

1949

GEORGE R. BENTLEY
FATHER VINCENT TEGEDER

1950
WILLIAM T. HAGAN

1951
JOHN F. STOVER

1953
PALMER H. BOEGER
LARRY GARA
WILLIAM H. RUSSELL
DAVID L. SMILEY
RICHARD D. YOUNGER
ROMAN J. ZORN

1955
SAM ROSS

1956
DONALD R. McNEIL

1957
FRANK L. BYRNE
CLIFFORD S. GRIFFIN

1958
P. J. STAUDENRAUS

1959
CLEMENT M. SILVESTRO
W. FLETCHER THOMPSON, JR.

1963
STEPHEN E. AMBROSE

1965
GORDON E. PARKS